*Contemporary
Austrian Poetry*

Contemporary Austrian Poetry

AN ANTHOLOGY

Edited and Translated by BETH BJORKLUND

Rutherford • Madison • Teaneck
Fairleigh Dickinson University Press
London and Toronto: Associated University Presses

Associated University Presses
440 Forsgate Drive
Cranbury, NJ 08512

Associated University Presses
25 Sicilian Avenue
London WC1A 2QH, England

Associated University Presses
2133 Royal Windsor Drive
Unit 1
Mississauga, Ontario
Canada L5J 1K5

*The paper used in this publication meets the
requirements of the American National Standard for
Permanence of Paper for Printed Library Materials
Z39.48-1984.*

Library of Congress Cataloging-in-Publication Data
Main entry under title:

Contemporary Austrian poetry.

Includes index.
1. German poetry—Austrian authors—Translations
into English.   2. German poetry—20th century—Trans-
lations into English.   3. English poetry—Translations
from German.   I. Bjorklund, Beth.
PT3824.Z5C6   1986   831'.914'08   84-46116
ISBN 0-8386-3178-9

Printed in the United States of America

Contents

When a person writes
It wants to reveal itself as progress
The house is closed
The night in which one re-reads the sentences
"These poems were anticipations"

Foreword

That Austria has not been merely an appendage to literature written in German, overshadowed by the imagination and poetic fervor of its inventive neighbor to the north, is clear from this immense collection of poetry by Austrians in translation by Beth Bjorklund. The fifty-five poets presented here—ranging in age from eighty-seven to thirty-nine—represent a vivid cross-section and panorama of Austrian lyric efforts in the twentieth century, particularly in the third quarter of that period.

Austria is not alone in being the homeland of a mixture of traditional and innovative poetic styles, structure, and content. But Austria may be unique in being able to harbor hidebound traditionalists along with exuberant experimentalists, though, admittedly, the two camps do not always (actually seldom) get along artistically and personally. In her collection of representative poets and lyrical expression Dr. Bjorklund demonstrates, however, that traditionalists and experimentalists sit well together, that the texture of poetic Austria would be incomplete without the contributions of both.

An observant reader will note immediately that the present volume affords easy access to a review and overview of trends that have marked Austrian poetry in the last few decades. The pioneering and influential experimental works of the so-called Viennese Group, from 1958 onward, ended the paramount role of the traditional poets. And the later contributions of the "Forum Stadtpark" poets centered in Graz brought that city into the mainstream of poetic invention and expression.

Readers will note further that poets increasingly have begun to question their roles in society and to express skepticism about the very tool of their trade, language itself. That sort of creative doubt has been endemic in the twentieth century in almost all literatures, and that of Austria is no exception. The irony is that poets express their doubts eloquently; their deliberate, outspoken consideration of what poetry is, what a poem is, what writing poetry means—and several poets here indulge in such reflection— forms a welcome and interesting definition of the poetic act and its result.

The poet writing in Austria—or, increasingly, the Austrian poet writing outside Austria, usually in West Germany—does not work in provincial isolation. The readership of poets writing in a language native to four nations—East and West Germany, Switzerland, and Austria—is broader than the population of the poet's native land. Austrian poets are published, too, not only in Austria but more and more outside Austria, particularly in West Germany. Austrian publishers who devote part of their lists to poets are relatively few in number, but the poet is presented to the public in lively literary periodicals as well.

Of the fifty-five poets included in this volume, probably not more than twenty are well known outside Austria. The editor and translator of the volume has done readers an incomparable favor by including lesser-known poets whose voices are just as compelling, whose themes are as riveting as those of their better-known compatriots. There is no sameness here in form or content. On the contrary, a variety of personal encounters with living, expressed through the lyrical mode, distinguishes this collection. The reader of the volume will no doubt embark on a personal voyage of exploration, wishing to read more of this poet or that, wishing to learn how various poets further come to grips with quite personal as well as universal passions and pursuits and encounters with individuals, institutions, and society as a whole.

The energy and skill of the editor/translator, Dr. Bjorklund, and the envious breadth of her familiarity with Austrian poetry of our own day, command respect and admiration. And our gratitude.

A. Leslie Willson

Acknowledgments

For permission to publish translations from the works listed below, I gratefully acknowledge the following publishers and authors.

Ilse Aichinger, *Verschenkter Rat* © 1978, S. Fischer Verlag, Frankfurt am Main.

René Altmann, in *protokolle*, © 1979, by Mrs. Altmann.

h. c. artmann, *ein lilienweißer brief aus lincolnshire* © 1969, Suhrkamp Verlag, Frankfurt am Main.

Rose Ausländer, *Gesammelte Gedichte* © 1977, S. Fischer Verlag, Frankfurt am Main.

Ingeborg Bachmann, *Werke I* © 1978, R. Piper & Co. Verlag, München.

Konrad Bayer, *Das Gesamtwerk* © 1977, Rowohlt Verlag, Reinbek bei Hamburg, by Mrs. Traudl Bayer.

Rudolf Bayr, *Der Wolkenfisch* © 1964, Residenz Verlag, Salzburg.

Gerald Bisinger, *7 Gedichte zum Vorlesen* © 1968, Literarisches Colloquium, Berlin.

Christine Busta, *Lampe und Delphin* © 1955, Otto Müller Verlag, Salzburg. *Unterwegs zu älteren Feuern* © 1965, Otto Müller Verlag, Salzburg. *Salzgärten* © 1975, Otto Müller Verlag, Salzburg.

Paul Celan, *Mohn und Gedächtnis* © 1952, Deutsche Verlags-Anstalt, Stuttgart. *Von Schwelle zu Schwelle* © 1955, Deutsche Verlags-Anstalt, Stuttgart. *Sprachgitter* © 1959, S. Fischer Verlag, Frankfurt am Main. *Die Niemandsrose* © 1963, S. Fischer Verlag, Frankfurt am Main. *Atemwende* © 1967, Suhrkamp Verlag, Frankfurt am Main. *Fadensonnen* © 1968, Suhrkamp Verlag, Frankfurt am Main. *Lichtzwang* © 1970, Suhrkamp Verlag, Frankfurt am Main. *Schneepart* © 1971, Suhrkamp Verlag, Frankfurt am Main. *Zeitgehöft* © 1976, Suhrkamp Verlag, Frankfurt am Main.

Ernst David, *Erfahrungen* © 1976, Verlag G. Grasl, Baden bei Wien.

Klaus Demus, *Morgennacht* © 1969, Günther Neske Verlag, by the author. *Das Morgenleuchten* © 1979, Günther Neske Verlag, by the author. *Schatten vom Wald* © 1983, Günther Neske Verlag, by the author.

Jeannie Ebner, *Gedichte* © 1965, by the author.

Erich Fried, *Anfechtungen* © 1967, Verlag Klaus Wagenbach, Berlin. *Die Freiheit den Mund aufzumachen* © 1972, Verlag Klaus Wagenbach, Berlin.

Barbara Frischmuth, in *manuskripte*, © 1982, by the author.

Gerhard Fritsch, *Gesammelte Gedichte* © 1978, Otto Müller Verlag, Salzburg.

Hermann Gail, *Weiter Herrschaft der weissen Mäuse* © 1979, Verlag G. Grasl, Baden bei Wien.

Elfriede Gerstl, *spielräume* © 1977, edition neue texte, Linz.

Alfred Gesswein, *Beton wächst schneller als Gras* © 1977, Delp'sche Verlagsbuchhandlung, München. *Zielpunkte* © 1977, Verlag G. Grasl, Baden bei Wien. *Vermessenes Gebiet* © 1967, Otto Müller Verlag, Salzburg.

Alfred Gong, *Gnadenfrist* © 1980, Verlag G. Grasl, Baden bei Wien.

Michael Guttenbrunner, *Ungereimte Gedichte* © 1959, claassen verlag, Düsseldorf. *Gesang der Schiffe* © 1980, claassen verlag, Düsseldorf.

Peter Handke, *Das Ende des Flanierens* © 1980, Suhrkamp Verlag, Frankfurt am Main.

Peter Henisch, *mir selbst auf der spur* © 1977, Verlag G. Grasl, Baden bei Wien.

Alois Hergouth, *Flucht zu Odysseus* © 1975, Verlag Styria, Graz. *Schwarzer Tribut* © 1958, Leykam Buchverlagsgesellschaft, Graz.

Max Hölzer, *Gesicht ohne Gesicht* © 1968, S. Fischer Verlag, by the author. *Mare occidentis. Das verborgene Licht. Chrysopöe* © 1976, Verlag Günther Neske, by the author.

Ernst Jandl, *Der künstliche Baum* © 1970, Hermann Luchterhand Verlag, Darmstadt. *dingfest* © 1973, Hermann Luchterhand Verlag, Darmstadt. *für alle* © 1974, Hermann Luchterhand Verlag, Darmstadt. *Laut und Luise* © 1976, Philipp Reclam, by the author. *sprechblasen* © 1979, Philipp Reclam, by the author.

Kurt Klinger, *Löwenköpfe* © 1977, Verlag G. Grasl, Baden bei Wien. *Auf dem Limes* © 1980, Otto Müller Verlag, Salzburg.

Alfred Kolleritsch, *Einübung in das Vermeidbare* © 1978, Residenz Verlag, Salzburg.

Hertha Kräftner, *Das Werk* © 1977, Edition Roetzer Gesellschaft, Eisenstadt.

Otto Laaber, *Inventur* © 1976, Verlag G. Grasl, Baden bei Wien.

Christine Lavant, *Kunst wie meine ist nur verstümmeltes Leben* © 1978, Otto Müller Verlag, Salzburg.

Friederike Mayröcker, *Ausgewählte Gedichte* © 1979, Suhrkamp Verlag, Frankfurt am Main. *Gute Nacht, guten Morgen* © 1982, Suhrkamp Verlag, Frankfurt am Main.

Erika Mitterer, *Klopfsignale* © 1970, Jugend und Volk Verlagsgesellschaft, Wien. *Entsühnung des Kain* © 1974, Johannes Verlag, Einsiedeln. Erika Mitterer, Rainer Maria Rilke, *Briefwechsel in Gedichten mit Erika Mitterer* © 1950, Suhrkamp Verlag, Frankfurt am Main.

Doris Mühringer, *Gedichte II* © 1969, Österreichische Verlagsanstalt, Wien. *Staub öffnet das Auge* © 1976, Verlag Styria, Graz.

Karl Wawra, *Die Auferstehung der Sonnenblume* © 1968, Bergland Verlag, Wien, by the author.

Juliane Windhager, *Schnee-Erwartung* © 1979, Residenz Verlag, Salzburg.

Herbert Zand, *Aus zerschossenem Sonnengeflecht* © 1973, Europaverlag, Wien.

Peter Zumpf, *Klärungen* © 1980, Verlag G. Grasl, Baden bei Wien.

Joachim Schondorff, ed., *Zeit und Ewigkeit* © 1978, claassen verlag, Düsseldorf.

Podium, Verlag G. Grasl, Baden bei Wien.

Some of the translations have appeared in the following journals: *The Literary Review, Denver Quarterly, Modern Poetry in Translation, Dimension, Micromegas, Affinities, Paintbrush.*

Introduction

Postwar Austrian Poetry

Beth Bjorklund

WHAT GEORGE BERNARD SHAW said about England and the United States is applicable to Austria and Germany: they are separated by the same language. Attempts at characterizing German and Austrian "national consciousness" range from Hofmannsthal's essay on "Prussians and Austrians" in 1917 to the popular reversal of a myth: in Berlin things are serious but not hopeless, whereas in Vienna they are hopeless but not serious. In the endlessly interesting debate on the issue of national literatures, critics have tried—and usually failed—to isolate characteristics that would differentiate Austrian literature from that of other German-speaking countries. A more fruitful approach would be to begin with the differing political, religious, and cultural traditions whence the literature stems; one could then look for manifestations of these differences in the respective literatures.

Austrians have been proud of their one-thousand-year-old Danubian culture of multiple nationalities. In fact, according to some observers, they are still trying to recover from the shock of loss. The Hapsburg Empire, beginning in 1278 and extending until 1918, established a strong sense of continuity of tradition, with Vienna as the capital. The effectiveness of the Counter Reformation insured the dominance of the Roman Catholic Church and gave rise to a rich Baroque culture of lasting significance. The geographic location in Middle Europe made the Monarchy a meeting place between East and West. It was a veritable melting pot of ethnic elements—Germanic, Magyar, Slavic, Jewish, and Romance peoples—united by a supranational Hapsburg culture. The composite character of the multilingual Empire, the conservative influence of the Catholic Church, and the underlying tensions of the Baroque culture are some of the chief factors that shaped the tradition.

The eve of the Monarchy was, paradoxically, a high point of cultural achievement, and Austria at this time produced some of its primary contri-

An earlier form of this essay appeared in *World Literature Today* 55 (1981). Copyright 1981 by the University of Oklahoma Press.

butions to Western civilization. In music, art, and literature, as well as in philosophy, psychology, and the natural sciences, the age proved rich on invention.[1] The *fin de siècle* atmosphere gave rise to the myth of "Gay Vienna"; and it also provided the scene for Freud's analysis of both "civilization" and its "discontents." (While psychological observation has always been more appealing to Austrians than philosophical abstraction, it has also been said that Vienna was the city where psychoanalysis needed to be invented!) Age-old questions of appearance and reality manifested themselves as problems of language and consciousness, and the tradition of language criticism was further developed by Mauthner, Karl Kraus, and Wittgenstein. In literature the early part of the century produced such renowned figures as Rilke, Hofmannsthal, Trakl, Kafka, Musil, Broch, Doderer, and Canetti. Impressionism was a strong movement, often coupled with symbolism and neo-romanticism; this was followed by expressionism and later surrealism. The demise of the Monarchy and the instability of the Second Republic led to social upheaval and the cataclysmic events of the Nazi regime. The situation in 1945 at the end of the war is commonly recognized as a "zero point."

The "presence of the past," as Hofmannsthal said, and the relationship to tradition are crucial issues in Austrian thought. Awareness of the cultural heritage results in a unqiue form of modern sensibility: on the one hand is a tendency to relativize the present in order to conserve the past; on the other hand is a reaction against the past in an effort to change the present. In the themes as well as forms of literature, convention and innovation interact to produce a redefinition of received structures and a reformulation of old questions in accordance with the changing attitudes of present-day society.

Postwar Austrian poetry is characterized by two main lines of development: the "traditional" and the "experimental"; to this can be added a third category, as represented by the most recent, "post-experimental," writing. Generalization, however, necessarily entails distortion, and thus the categories must not be viewed as restrictive, nor the classes as homogeneous, for many viable modes exist within the groupings. Neither is the system evaluative, since continuity does not preclude invention any more than change necessarily entails originality. Tradition is, of course, a multifaceted affair, and the effects depend upon which traditions are appealed to and how they are actualized. The question of adherence to or departure from traditions remains, however, a crucial issue, which perhaps only demonstrates the strength and significance of the underlying concerns.

I

The literary scene in postwar occupied Austria was dominated by traditional interests, as writers reviewed recent developments and rediscovered an individual voice after the collective world disaster. Poets in search of models often looked back to Hofmannsthal, Rilke, and Weinheber. The most prominent poets of the postwar period, Celan and Bachmann, lived outside Austria, in Paris and Rome, respectively, where each surpassed regional restrictions to produce a literature worthy of world renown. At home the state-supported PEN Club, as well as small magazines and literary circles, fulfilled the necessary function of creating a forum for writers, the conservative hegemony of which lasted into the mid-1950s.

As representative of a traditional stance, Christine Busta presents a type of "modern classicism." Her six lyric volumes have met with a warm reception and have undergone multiple printings during the past three decades. Whereas this may say something about the Austrian reading public, which is generally conservative, it is also indicative of the accessibility of her poetry and the strength of the experiential conviction conveyed therein. Thematically, her works embody traditional concerns of nature, religion, humanity, and existential quest, and formally they participate in the postwar development toward reduction of form and concentration of image. Consider, for example, the following poem:

Salt Gardens

Above dried-up
river beds
the phoenix flower
blooms invisibly
out of the white
ashes of the sea.

Salzgärten (1975)

Not only have rhyme and regularity of rhythm disappeared, but gone also are the decorative modifiers and, in some cases, the syntactic cohesion of traditional verse. The result is increased power of metaphor, which succeeds here by its apparent simplicity.

Metaphor is central also to the poetry of Christine Lavant, who is frequently associated with Busta, however diverse their poetry may be. Lavant often employs conventional rhyme and rhythmic patterns to articulate a highly individual form of religious mysticism, with images of fear and suffering evoking a visionary realm of redemption:

I asked the headless snake
and dipped my hands in the moon-blood;
now I go to heal the unlucky star
so that it can ascend again

before my hands betray it.
The hill lifts me up a bit,
in the moon-blood I see the mirror of the sea;
there the star cowers in a coral reef
and calls for help like a bird. . . .

Kunst wie meine ist nur verstümmeltes Leben (1978)

Metaphor, as exemplified in the works of Busta and Lavant, represents one of the main strengths of traditional poetry, and it is also an important point of departure for later developments. The question of metaphor is, in fact, central enough to serve as basis for comparison, since the function assigned to metaphoric speaking implies an attitude toward language and what language can or cannot accomplish. The efficacy of poetic speaking is indeed a central concern of modern poetry.

Focus on the (in-)adequacy of language is paradigmatically represented by the two leading poets of the period, Ingeborg Bachmann and Paul Celan. Bachmann's reputation as a poet rests on two volumes, *Die gestundete Zeit* (1953; Borrowed Time) and *Anrufung des grossen Bären* (1956; Invocation of the Great Bear). The works present extravagant pictorial evocations of the existential themes of time and consciousness, with poetry functioning as a summons to lucid wakefulness and moral sensitivity. Although many of the poems take love as their topic, communication of any sort reveals itself to be impossible in the wasteland of the modern ice age. A benumbed sense of isolation leads to a questioning of the effectiveness of the poetic word, as exemplified in "Word and Afterword":

Come, favor of sound and breath,
strengthen this mouth
when its weakness
horrifies and hinders us.

Come and don't fail,
since we are at war with so much wrong.
Before dragon blood protects the enemy
this hand will pass through the fire.
My Word, deliver me!

Anrufung des grossen Bären

A type of language crisis ensued, comparable to that of Hofmannsthal's "Lord Chandos Letter" half a century earlier. Bachmann subsequently gave up writing poetry and turned to prose.

Similar themes are present in the work of Celan, who developed them further to the logical—and radical—conclusion of "absolute metaphor."

Celan's oeuvre comprises nine volumes of poetry, from *Mohn und Gedächtnis* (1952; Poppy and Memory) through *Sprachgitter* (1959; Language Lattice) to the posthumous volumes after his suicide in 1970. Often regarded as representative for the postwar period is his widely anthologized piece "Todesfuge" (Fugue of Death), written in 1945:[2]

> Black milk of the morning we drink it at evening
> we drink it at noon and at dawn we drink it at night
> we drink and we drink
> we dig a grave in the sky there's plenty of room there
> A man lives in the house he plays with his snakes he writes
> he writes when night falls on Germany your golden hair
>   Margarite
> he writes it and steps out of the house and stars shine he calls
>   for his hounds
> he calls for his Jews to come dig a grave in the ground
> he commands us play a song for the dance . . .

Mohn und Gedächtnis

The poem occupies the place among Celan's works that "Guernica" does among Picasso's: a formal masterpiece in a radically modern idiom with overt reference to forces that shaped the artist's life, as well as the course of history. Through a language as metaphorically concentrated as it is mystically associative, Celan attempts to transcend the logical limits of experience, and the receding utterance of the late poems can be viewed as an attempt to articulate thought apart from the referential character of language.

To this allegedly "extreme" position of linguistic and existential questioning Erich Fried reacted with an ostensibly "traditional" humanistic argument, as follows:

Upon Re-reading a Poem by Paul Celan

"there are
still songs to be sung beyond
humanity"*

. . .
Songs
certainly
also beyond
our death
Songs of the future
beyond the terrible times
in which we are entangled

A singing beyond
the humanly conceivable
Vast

But not a single song
beyond humanity

Die Freiheit, den Mund aufzumachen (1972)
*From a Celan poem in *Atemwende* (1967)

Fried's position is that of an Austrian poet living in London who has maintained literary and political engagement over the past three decades. Although he experiments with language, he does not question its communicative power, but rather uses it to express sociopolitical convictions.

Another response to the questions posed by Celan's poetry—his life and his death, which in its extremity so shook the literary world—is illustrated by Doris Mühringer's "On the Death of Paul Celan (A Vindication)":

Again one
Again one of the seismographs
of the world
overladen
We should acquire
more callous
antennae
We should become
more robust
instruments
But
should we?

Staub öffnet das Auge (1976)

Michael Guttenbrunner, heir and elegist on the one hand, and critic and activist on the other, is also highly conscious of the dichotomies of the age, as exemplified ironically in "Return":

Much happens in silence,
when the storm cries itself red
or the stars shine angrily.
Oh, then the street chokes
on the deaf stones,
and the scream of the step spins around,
and grief wails up through the cracks.

Don't touch it!

Suppress the terrible sound!
Return to the rose
of an earlier time,
when you, as shepherd,
called into the valley of desire,
and the sheep came to you.

Opferholz (1954)

II

In the early fifties a different kind of literature, termed "experimental," was introduced by the so-called "Vienna Group." The movement was initiated by h. c. artmann, and it consisted later of Friedrich Achleitner, Konrad Bayer, Gerhard Rühm and Oswald Weiner, who worked collectively and individually for over a decade. The "revolt" began in 1953 with artmann's "Eight-Point Proclamation of the Poetic Act," which opens with the following provocative statement: "One can be a poet without ever having written a word."[3] Writers *cum* actors drew on the traditions of surrealism and Dada, with elements also from the baroque *commedia dell'arte*, magic theater, and black humor. Innovation was of highest priority, functioning as criticism of received standards of aesthetics and ethics. The experimental stance questioned the very presuppositions of art, language, and society. The movement was received better abroad, in Germany and Switzerland, than at home in Vienna, where anarchy was feared, and bristling debate ensued.

The problem of language was of central concern to the experimentalists. At stake was the question of whether or not reality was being distorted in some insidious manner by the linguistic means used to evoke it. The experimentalists *cum* writers were opposed to symbol and metaphor, regarding it as a mask for phony metaphysics. Their intent was rather to strip language of its mythology and mysticism by reducing it to the material substance which it, in fact, is. Language bits could then serve as raw material, like the painter's colors or the musician's sounds, for new possibilities of combination. Reconstruction resulted in forms of montage and collage, permutation and dislocation, kaleidoscopic constellations, serial constructions, and chains of nonreferential associations. The mimetic intent of traditional literature was thus radically redefined and a speech created commensurate with a different level of reality.

It was through this channel that linguistic dialects were introduced into modern non-naive poetry. The dialect poems of artmann, as well as his "minstrel" lyrics, were popular with the public and served also as seminal for other writers. In general, however, the atomization of language met with widespread misunderstanding, if not downright disapproval, and in retro-spect the movement was more important for its liberating effects than for any lasting monuments. It was not until the early sixties that the spirit of innovation achieved a broader basis and the literary scene truly changed.

Exploitation of the material properties of language led to the so-called "concrete poetry," an international phenomenon to which Austria, as well as Switzerland, has richly contributed with the well-known names of Ernst Jandl and Eugen Gomringer. Jandl has a wide range of serious and not-so-serious styles, some of which are predominantly acoustic, some visual, as in the poem reproduced in part below (English original):

BIOGRAPHY


```
d      eat      h
d      eat      h
 d     eat   h
  d    eat h
  death
```

COMING . . .

```
 earth
e  art h
 e   art  h
e    art     h
e    art     h
```

. . . AND GOING

(*Der künstliche Baum*, 1970)

The title is, of course, a spoof on conventional personalized forms, and the horizontal, vertical, and diagonal patterns of expansion and contraction engage the viewer in various planes of relations. Indeed, participatory poet-ics is one of the strengths of concrete poetry, for its openness not only invites but requires response by the reader to complete the meaning of the poem.

Associated with Jandl through friendship and collaboration is Friederike Mayröcker, a prolific writer of both prose and poetry. Her leading lyric volume, *Tod durch Musen* (1966; Death by the Muses), demonstrates an imaginative and radical use of metaphor. Whereas metaphoric vision is tradi-tionally analogical, here it is most often disjunctive. Narrative content is largely replaced by verbal pattern, with language referring to itself as much as to any external phenomena. Titles themselves are illustrative, such as "Sad Text with Tongue-Glue," which opens as follows:

Bachofen (Johann, Jakob) Tranquille seam-soul lark-gray;
    larch-green
circles by Dada work-flat insufficient and werewolfish
round-bearded (Sundays) around the Moor-chain on the neck of
    his daughter . . .

(Tod durch Musen)

Regarded as more accessible is her early work, as represented by the widely-anthologized piece, "what I call you / when I think about you / and you are not there," which consists of a long list of epithets, ranging from "my wild strawberry" to "my backwards counter." Also from her early work is the poem "Will wither like grass," which stands as a memorial to Brahms's "German Requiem."

Mayröcker and Jandl have collaborated in innovatively redefining the genre of the *Hörspiel* (radio play), which has a venerable tradition in modern German literature. In the hands of these authors the radio play gives up its "story" element and becomes an acoustic montage, similar in effect to a performance of poetry. In fact, we as readers may be making sharper—i.e., more traditional—distinctions than the authors themselves are willing to make. Modern writers, eschewing the ideology attached to inherited forms, often prefer to designate their work with the neutral nomenclature of "text," emphasizing also the materiality of the art object. Genre definitions are indeed called into question as contemporary poetry assumes the form of a visual or acoustic collage or employs non-causal, non-referential linguistic strategies for an "unpoetic" statement.

There followed in the wake of Jandl, Mayröcker, and the Vienna Group a second generation of poets for whom experimentation served as a springboard for various concerns. The initial departure from tradition encouraged a group of younger writers, together with musicians and visual artists, to found the "Forum City Park" in Graz in 1959–60. This event is commonly recognized as a turning point, and "the history of the 'Forum Stadtpark' is the history of modern Austrian literature."[4] Conceived as an alternative to the PEN Club in Vienna, the Graz group took an oppositional stance and became known as "Anti-PEN." The movement gained momentum, with its quarterly journal *manuskripte* and its annual arts festival, "Steirischer Herbst" (Styrian Fall), and developed in 1973 into the "Grazer Autorenversammlung" GAV (Graz Writers' Association). The group is characterized more by common interests and cooperative undertakings than by any unified poetic program. Writing is, in fact, highly diverse. Among the various concerns, two main lines are discernible: on the one hand a linguistic branch, which carries the innovations of the Vienna group to their logical conclusion; on the other hand a sociopolitical branch, which includes Marxism and Feminism (although political activism of the sort present in West Germany remains foreign to Austria).

As representative of linguistic interests, Reinhard Priessnitz is a serious young poet with a strong theoretical interest in literature. (In this he is somewhat alone, since Austrians are less inclined to theory-building than their German colleagues.) Priessnitz's work can be viewed as an implementation of Wittgenstein's language criticism. Distrustful of the camouflaging effect of standard metaphor, he instead operates with other levels of language and creates metaphors with phonetic, rhythmic, and syntactic patterns. The "message" in his poems is communicated on non-semantic levels, whereby unreadability itself becomes a theme of the poem:

> "white horse song"
>
> white clock (?) white commu
> nion(?) or when everything (?)
> is revealed thus questions (?) &
> early & the last face is ex
> tinguished (?) with that what i
> say say with that what i
> . . .

vierundvierzig gedichte (1978)

Understood was only Preissnitz's "Luciferian" intent, and his radical stance met with opposition from both the right and the left.[5] Traditionalists found it to be "nonsense," and activists called it "elitist." His visual and acoustic experiments are, however, not so arbitrary as they may initially appear but serve rather to challenge the epistemology behind the structures.

The work of Heidi Pataki illustrates the sociocultural position of a young writer with the dual concerns of language and society:

nature morte

> who has you then you pretty wood?
> and when? and why? how long? how soon?
> a hoar-frost fell? "strawberry fields"?
> one says? may be? and nice good night?
> do you have words? never yet heard?
> did you not promise? this and that? . . .

Schlagzeilen (1968)

Her later ironic-satiric poems in *stille post* (1978) present a montage of literary snippets plundered from the Classic-Romantic tradition of German literature. Lines from Goethe, Rilke, and others are arranged in interrogative or exclamatory form, interwoven with banal slogans and slang phrases. The mixture is then cast in virtuoso rhythmic and stanzaic schemes, whereby speech patterns are de-masked as manifestations of behavioral conditioning. In this cliché-ridden world, where individuality and authenticity are mere anachronisms, the crass juxtaposition of disparate elements reveals the paradox of modern poetry and questions the possibility of personal meaning. The intentionally provocative nature of *stille post* is further illustrated by accompanying photographs of the author—naked.

The foregoing discussion has attempted to present the broad spectrum— allowing for intermediary gradations—of postwar poetry. It is, of course, no coincidence that traditionalists and experimentalists often belong to different generations, and a "gap" is commonly asserted. There are, however, enough counter-examples to prevent the use of age as an explanatory factor. The generation of poets born in the 1920s constitutes half the authors represented here. In contrast to their predecessors, who had characterized themselves as the "lost generation" of the war years, these writers, who were young adults when the war ended, produced a significant contribution to modern literature. Women too have played a prominent role in the literary life of the past three decades, without necessarily espousing a "feminism." Again, however, there are no inherent correlations, and one finds instead many cross-overs between sex and age of an author and mode of writing.

III

If the sixties was a decade of opposition, the early seventies saw the culmination of conflict as well as something of a resolution. Fronts have largely been overcome or abandoned, and poets in both camps, as well as in many intermediary positions, continue to write. This leads to a third and new category of writers who published their first lyric volumes in the seventies. Although one would not view the category as a synthesis (which is probably not possible), it represents a suspension of old oppositions by the discovery of a new lyric voice. Innovation came by re-phrasing or totally by-passing the old issues, and what emerged are two "postexperimental" strains, overlapping rather than mutually exclusive. They can be informally designated as an interest in the reflexivity and self-referentiality of language and, secondly, a concern with the subjectivity of experience.

Jutta Schutting's interest in language is clearly of a different order from that of the sixties, and in the Austrian tradition of language criticism, she uses language to question its own premises. New is the topicalization of this in a poem, which, in its metalinguistic commentary, turns back on itself to investigate the conditions of its own existence. The resulting analytic construct concerns basic questions of reality and identity, the relationship between word and object, and the nature of metaphoric transformation. The poet's ritualistic process of naming is followed by interrogation of the meaning of the activity. The outcome is an anti-nominalist position, although this is not without recognizing the ever-present danger of reductionism, as indicated by the conclusion of the poem below:

Doves

I fed this dove
when the word dove had become something without reference to
   real doves
and this one when the word in a poem
was a synonym for message
and this one when in a love poem
a dove in the last line was something different from the dove in the
   first line
. . . . . .
and this one
when the word in a poem
was for me an evasion and idle enchantment

(In der Sprache der Inseln; 1973)

If the cleft between language and experience was always problematic, the tension is here heightened by the objectivity of the form in relation to the intensity of the emotion. The reflective mode of awareness and self-consciousness is far from traditional metaphoric usage, as writing loses its sense of spontaneity and naïveté and becomes increasingly the topic of its own activity. This is often accompanied by an emphasis on the writing process as such, and for some poets the process even seems to take precedence over the finished product. The self-referentiality has, of course, many parallels in other genres and other literatures, with analogies also to poststructuralist criticism, although questions of influence remain delicate and dangerous. One is, however, reminded of Roland Barthes' essay entitled "To Write: An Intransitive Verb?".[6] The title could serve as emblematic for the contemporary movement that takes as its chief concern the cognitive inquiry of language.

   Poetry of subjectivity entails no lesser degree of awareness, but the focus is more on experience than on language, and particularly on the highly individual, inward nature of experience, with obvious parallels to the so-called "new subjectivity" trend in recent literature in West Germany. The genre is most prominently represented by Alfred Kolleritsch, who in 1978 received the coveted Petrarca Prize for his lyric volume *Einübung in das Vermeidbare*

(1978; Exercise in the Avoidable). It was only the fourth time that the Petrarca Prize had been awarded, and the ceremony in Siena, to which Peter Handke gave the laudatory,[7] received wide coverage in the European press. The prize is not only one of the most prestigious awards, with its exotic foreign flair, but it also carries the largest monetary compensation of any literary award in the German-speaking countries, and was, for any or all of these reasons, dubbed by the press a "sensuous" Nobel Prize. "Hardworking," however, rather than "epicurean," was the image of the author in the eyes of the public, for he is a well-known, active figure on the current literary scene.

Kolleritsch's award-winning poetry is pitched in a distinctly low key, with an ironic idiom of understatement. A conversational-narrative voice telescopes the complex emotions into metaphors as unusual and opaque as the sensations they were meant to convey. The cycle of untitled poems presents the cognitive-emotive process of encountering and questioning the self in its personal identity as well as its interpersonal relations. The framework is a love relationship, and the motif of separation runs as an undercurrent throughout. A high degree of self-awareness, however, separates this poetry from that of naïve response. Realistic elements are present, but the work is more an examination of consciousness and its manifestations than of a love relationship as empirical phenomenon. Boundaries between subject and object become blurred as perception becomes increasingly problematic, and just as there are no "neutral" events, neither is there any "objective" world. Remaining is only the individual with its subjective responses. The resulting isolation and anxiety give rise to a vigilance wary of any security system:

> We remember only that
> which leaves behind images,
> we drive experiences
> together into chains
> and exhaustedly acknowledge
> how unified we are . . .

> *Einübung in das Vermeidbare*

The dominant chord of skepticism is set by the opening line of the cycle: "I don't trust my impressions." It is the poetic unpacking of the implications of this statement that constitutes Kolleritsch's outstanding achievement.

The literature of subjectivity has been sharply criticized for its alleged narcissistic concerns.[8] The debate in West Germany centered on the nature of the dialectical relations in the process of self-objectification and on the kind and degree of subjectivity requisite to a true sense of objectivity. Defenders maintain that the so-called "questions of the age" are displaced forms of dissatisfaction with the self and that the latter is the proper starting point for investigation. From a historical perspective, the "inward turn" can be regarded as a reaction against the call to activism of political poetry; analogously, the "banality" of subject matter can be seen as a reaction against the "profundity" of the hermetic tradition. Whether one is left with a viable topic is an issue that will be resolved largely by one's prior assumptions concerning the nature and function of literature. The movement can in any case be regarded as an attempt to bring together literature and life, to find a middle way between the "elitism" of *poésie pure* and the "populism" of *poésie engagée.*

Questions of language and consciousness thus constitute some of the central concerns of contemporary Austrian poetry, and they are indicative also of relationships between Austrian literature and that of West Germany and other European nations. Not thereby eclipsed are the many other themes and modes of writing that remain open today as viable alternatives. Pluralism is indeed the policy of the Austrian Society for Literature, which, since its founding two decades ago, has done much to mediate disputes and promote both the production and reception of literature. An egalitarian tendency is evidenced also by the appearance of five anthologies in recent years, including two East German collections of Austrian literature.[9] The most grandiose project, namely the anthology *Zeit und Ewigkeit* (Time and Eternity), turned out to be a publishing disaster. A lengthy list of errata compiled by reviewers revealed the "scandal," and the edition was subsequently recalled and a new one issued in its place (not, however, without the original having become a collector's item with a market value!).

The ideology-loaded appellation "Time and Eternity" bears on the question of tradition, for the "Burden of the Past," to borrow another title, has been a central issue in the literary and cultural development of Austria in the postwar period. On the one hand stands the hallowed canon from Walther von der Vogelweide through Hofmannsthal. On the other hand, Austria, like other Western countries, has developed into an increasingly mechanized and computerized society in which poets strive for new modes of expression. The most interesting results may be those inclusive, yet open-ended works that capture the unresolved tensions in a double-sighted vision of both continuity and innovation.

Notes

1. Some of the leading works in English are as follows: Alan Janik and Stephen Toulmin, *Wittgenstein's Vienna* (New York: Simon & Schuster, 1973); William A. Johnston, *The Austrian Mind: An Intellectual and Social History, 1848–1938* (Berkeley and Los Angeles: University of California Press, 1971); Carl E. Schorske, *Fin-de-siècle Vienna: Politics and Culture* (New York: A. Knopf, 1980); in German see Ivar Ivask et al., *Das grosse Erbe* (Graz: Stiasny, 1962); Claudio Magris, *Der habsburgische Mythos in der österreichischen Literatur* (Salzburg: O. Müller, 1966).

2. See Karl S. Weimar, "Paul Celan's 'Todesfuge': Translation and Interpretation," PMLA 89 (1974): 85–96; L. L. Duroche, "Paul Celan's 'Todesfuge': A New Interpretation," MLN 82 (1967): 472–77.

3. h. c. artmann, "acht-punkte-proklamation des poetischen actes," in Die Wiener Gruppe, ed. Gerhard Rühm (Reinbek: Rowohlt, 1967), p. 9.

4. Hilde Spiel, Kindlers Literaturgeschichte der Gegenwart. Lyrik (Zürich: Kindler, 1976), III, 95.

5. See Reinhard Priessnitz, "tribut an die tradition. aspekte einer postexperimentellen literatur," in Wie die Grazer auszogen, die Literatur zu erobern, ed. P. Laemmle and J. Drews (München: dtv, 1979), pp. 126–52; Ulrich Greiner, Der Tod des Nachsommers (München: C. Hanser, 1979), pp. 199–210.

6. Roland Barthes, "To Write: An Intransitive Verb?" in The Structuralist Controversy, ed. R. Macksey and E. Donato (Baltimore: The Johns Hopkins Press, 1970), pp. 134–56.

7. Peter Handke, Das Ende des Flanierens (Frankfurt: Suhrkamp, 1980), pp. 135–45.

8. See Jörg Drews, "Selbsterfahrung und Neue Subjektivität in der Lyrik," as well as essays by L. Fischer, P. Stephan, and H. Zimmermann, all in Akzente 24 (1977); the essays are collected in Lyrik-Katalog Bundesrepublik, ed. Jan Hans et al. (München: Goldmann, 1979).

9. Dichtung aus Österreich. II Lyrik, ed. Eugen Thurnher (Wien: Österreichischer Bundesverlag, 1977); Österreich heute. Ein Lesebuch, ed. Georgina Baum et al. (East Berlin: Volk and Welt, 1979); Verlassener Horizont. Österreichische Lyrik aus vier Jahrzehnten, ed. Hugo Huppert and Roland Links (East Berlin: Volk und Welt, 1980); Zeit und Ewigkeit. Tausend Jahre österreichische Lyrik, ed. Joachim Schondorff (Düsseldorf: claassen, 1978); reviewed in Profil (1979), 66–67; Zwischenbilanz. Eine Anthologie österreichischer Gegenwartsliteratur, ed. Walter Weiss and Sigrid Schmid (Salzburg: Residenz, 1976; rpt., München: dtv, 1978).

Notes on Translation: Equivalence?

I

Surely the oldest platitude about translation asserts its impossibility; probably the second oldest concerns its historical inevitability—the necessity of each generation remaking its own text. From Martin Luther's wrestling with the unitive Word of St. John to the Faustian progression of *Wort—Sinn—Kraft—Tat*, from Keats's first looking into Chapman's Homer to multilingual writers and dual-language editions, translation represents a living dialectic. The necessity of translation arises most obviously from the plurality of languages. But one could also say it arises from the phenomenon of language itself, since language is already an abstraction, a system of signs or symbols distinct from the things in themselves. Translation is therefore only a provisional way of coming to terms with language, and a theory of translation presupposes a theory of language. Thinkers such as W. V. Quine, Walter Benjamin, and Jacques Derrida have addressed themselves to the theory of translation; at stake are basic epistemological issues of the ontology of language.[1]

A central question in this context concerns the relationship of the translation to the original. The term "equivalence" can be used only in a metaphorical sense, since, as any schoolchild raised on new math will attest, the qualities of an equivalence relationship—symmetry, reflexivity, transitivity—are inevitably lacking in a translation. A naturalistic, verification theory of language such as that proposed by Quine finds an "inscrutability of reference" and an "indeterminacy of translation," with the results always and only approximate and tentative. This is distinct from an idealistic and phenomenological theory of language, and Benjamin posits a "nucleus of pure language." Derrida questions the entire notion of representation in Western thought, whereby there is no "original" text, since language can communicate only itself. No sea-change is possible because everything in

I am grateful to the editors of *Language and Style* for permission to reprint part of my essay that appeared in another context in that journal (Vol. 16, 1983).

language is transformation. One is reminded of Mallarmé's absolute poem, which would be less the sum of its meanings than their source and secret essence. Borges said that in all of literature there can be nothing but rough drafts: the concept of a "definitive text" belongs only to religion or to fatigue.[2]

The most common function of language and thus also of translation is to convey information. For this purpose (the since notorious) automatic translation was invented, the machine being simply a dictionary that consults itself at very high speed. The purpose of poetry, however, is not solely to convey a message; that is often the least essential, most superficial aspect of literature, since semantic information is limited to precisely that and in any case represents only one level of a work of art. The translation of a literary work assumes an entirely different character from that of a nonliterary work. A comprehensive theory of literary translation presupposes—or entails—a theory of literature, including consideration of the nature, meaning, and value of the literary work. Translation thus understood becomes a metaphor for criticism: the translator is the model reader, and the translation is a "reading" in the sense of an interpretation of the text. Translation is the most common form of commentary, and the difference between translation and interpretation often depends on the strength of the equivalence suggested. Pound speaks of "interpretive translation" with the goal being "to show where the treasure lies." This he distinguishes from another sort that "is definitely making a new poem" and "falls simply in the domain of original writing."[3] Indeed, poems such as "Homage to Sextus Propertius" have been criticized—and praised—for being neither fish nor fowl. Like interpretation, translation presupposes an intimate acquaintance with and an affinity for the text on the part of the translator. The results are of various sorts, depending upon the degree of correspondence: metaphrase and paraphrase, imitation and adaptation, transformation and transposition, thematic variant, stylistic analogue, and travesty and parody.

Presupposing a theory of language and of literature, we come to the theory of poetry translation. It can be argued that there is no such thing as translation in the abstract. There is no systematic model for the transfer of meaning between languages, and a scientific theory entailing the usual requirements of generalization, falsifiability, and prediction is probably not possible. Since the nature of meaning involves formal and referential as well as emotive aspects, no single set of principles will solve all the problems. A theory of translation should account rather for the principles and strategies needed to approach such problems. All theories of translation, whether formal, hermeneutic, or pragmatic, seem to be only variants of a single, inescapable question: How can the elegant—or merely the adequate—translation be achieved? In what ways can or should "equivalence" be sought? Jakobson finds that "poetry by definition is untranslatable; only creative transposition is possible."[4] Others have been less sanguine on the matter. Surely, however, Dryden and Pope, Arnold, FitzGerald, and Lowell were not deluding themselves when they found a substance that translation could not dissipate. Skepticism is usually confined to the assertion of an irreconcilability between accuracy and all other desiderata, and a dichotomy is often made between fidelity and freedom, loyalty and liberty, the literalists and the spiritualists. This I find to be a spurious dichotomy (although I am not certain that my deeper interpretation of freedom will serve to reconcile the two). Fidelity is, of course, an economic, if not a moral, necessity; it does not, however, stand in antithetical relation to freedom, but the process of translation is rather more complex.

If we begin our brief considerations with the receiver and work backward, so to speak, it is evident that recent work in the reception of literature has also influenced translation theory. De Beaugrande's recent book examines the varying aims of translation in regard to the intended audience, and he makes a distinction between formal and pragmatic resemblance.[5] A translation that aims at formal resemblance seeks a text-oriented, a source-oriented equivalence; a translation that aims at pragmatic resemblance seeks a reader-oriented equivalence, a similarity of communicative function. The distinction is between a concept of meaning as a property of language and a concept of meaning as the effective purpose of an utterance. There is, I believe, much to be said for the latter view, since language is, first and foremost, a communicative event, and "meaning" is after all a mental, not a linguistic, phenomenon. A basic principle of communication theory states that a message must be made to fit the decoder's channel. A message exists as it is perceived, and it is always and only the version created by the hearer/reader. It is therefore not enough to transfer the content, but rather the message must be encoded so as to generate a similar response in the receptor language. The translator seeks precision not necessarily in the text but rather in the effects he produces, although these effects must originate from the text.

If this is acceptable as a valid (if partial) goal, the focus reverts to the producer of texts, that is, the translator, with the question of how communicative relevance is to be achieved. It is by now commonplace to insist that literary criticism entail submission to the work at hand; as Northrop Frye wrote: "Understanding begins in a complete surrender of the mind and senses to the impact of the work as a whole."[6] If this is true of interpretation, then how much more so of translation, which we have posited to be the most intense form of close reading, literally forcing exposure to probability and confrontation with ambiguity. What moves the translator is not a mimetic urge but rather an elective affinity. In a classic humanistic essay of the nineteenth century, Wilamowitz speaks of "metempsychosis," of the necessity of getting inside the central consciousness of the author by a kind of clairvoyance.[7] Whatever psychic processes this may imply for the translators—and they are often willing to comment on the needs and risks of impersonation—"this insinuation of self into otherness is the final secret of the translator's craft," as Steiner wrote.[8] The type of imagination requisite to the task has affinities with both author and audience and entails a Janus-faced empathy with both cultural milieus.

Knowledge of the original text is thus a necessary condition; but it is not a sufficient condition. "Meaning" in itself does not imply transferability. It is only when we apprehend the "meaning of meaning" that we understand fully, and it is this realization that makes restatement potentially possible. To translate a poem is to compose another poem, and the sole aim is to produce a successful poem, which is then a re-creation, not a reproduction. A good translation depends not primarily on the knowledge of the original language but on the translator's skill as a poet in his own language. It follows that only a "poet" can translate a poem (although his poetry production may be limited to translation). This is demonstrated by the fact that a poet who does not know the source language working together with a native informant regularly produces a product superior to that of a nonpoet or scholar who knows the language well but does not write poetry. W. H. Auden expressed an extreme form of this view: "It does not particularly matter if the translators have understood their originals correctly; often, indeed, misunderstanding is, from the point of view of the native writer, more profitable."[9] This may perhaps not be what is commonly understood by "translation," yet an entire range of possibilities is present and has been attempted. The translator may not know the source language well, but he must know the receiver language intimately and be able to use it artistically. The translated poem should read like a poem written in the target language, although because of its origin it may be different from any poem ever composed in that language. The translation may then influence the literary tradition of the receiver language, as is amply documented in the history of literature.

The translator inevitably imposes a personal style, although what was said earlier about a thorough understanding of and identification with the poem should prevent one from usurping the role of the author. The process is not one of translation by words or even by structural units, but rather something like this: decoding the meaning, transferring the content, and generating a similar message in the receptor language. It is thus a process of decomposition and recomposition. Hermann Broch wrote: "Ich habe niemals Sätze, sondern immer nur Gedanken und deren Sinn übersetzt."[10] One may recreate a poem close to or far from the original; either extreme or any intermediate position may be justified, provided it is skillfully done. If the translator has the skill to reproduce the rhythm and rhyme, then all the better; if the translator does not have the skill, then the translation will be more effective—and thus also more faithful—if equivalence is sought on other levels. It necessarily involves compensation and trade-off, and the good translator finds the mechanisms to produce maximally the effects intended by the original. The poet/critic Barnstone wrote: "Fidelity to the *quality* of the original is foremost,"[11] and if the new poem is not a good poem, then the translation is a betrayal. It is quality alone that determines the relative validity of the Italian pun: "traduttore–traditore" (translator–traitor).

Evaluation of translations remains a crucial and debatable issue, and various criteria have been proposed. It can with good reason be argued that a translation should be evaluated first on its own merits, on the basis of whether or not it is a successful poem in its own language. This does not, of course, resolve the problem of evaluation, but it does put it back where it belongs: in the realm of literary evaluation in general. The practice of publishers to print the original and the translation on facing pages may serve various purposes, but among them is not evaluation, since if the poem is a good poem, its correspondence or lack thereof to the original is a descriptive rather than an evaluative statement. Belitt wrote: "The effect of matching texts in parallel columns is to induce a positivism with regard to poetry that is both misleading and illusory."[12] It is no more possible to assign a single "correct" translation than it is to assign a single correct interpretation. The translator, as well as the critic, must be conscious of the degree of distance to the original at which he is working; this consciousness, plus the skill of putting it into words, is the prime determinant of the quality of the translation. Freedom is thus not synonymous with falsification, nor is fidelity identical with exactitude. Just as attempted literalness may in the end be falsifying, so also may faithfulness be achieved most adequately by freedom of invention. All combinations are possible, which is only to say that the issue of fidelity versus freedom has little to do with the question of the "truth" of a translation.

I have argued for a freedom on the linguistic, pragmatic level. The tricks of the trade, the various strategies for achieving equivalence and substitution, correspondence and contrast, replacement and adjustment, matching and counterparts are delineated quite adequately in books such as those by Nida and Levý.[13] On this level one cannot properly speak of a theory but rather of a procedure, which can be exemplified only in reference to a particular text. It is on this level that the craft of the translator shows itself; there are no important illusions about the process, and my intent is not to minimize the types of decisions that must be made in regard to the concrete art object. The poet/translator Gass wrote as follows:

> How political it all is anyway. The poet struggles to rule a nation of greedy self-serving malcontents; every idea, however tangential to the main theme it may have been initially, wants to submerge the central subject beneath its fructifying self as though each drizzle were scheming a forty days rain; every jig and trot desire to be the whole dance; every la-de-da

and line length, image, order, rhyme, variation and refrain, every well-mouthed vowel, dental click, silent design, represents a corporation, international cartel or union, a Pentagon or AMA, eager to turn the law toward its interests; every word wants a potency so supreme it will emasculate the others. . . . Thus the completed poem is a series of delicate adjudications, a peace created from contention.[14]

When one steps back for a moment to consider the activity, it becomes apparent that freedom on this level is not contradictory but rather subservient to a fidelity on a more abstract level. Sensitivity intensified becomes moral vision, an observation that led Walter Benjamin to posit the ideal translation as the most literal in the sense of being from "inside" the source. He wrote: "To some degree all great texts contain their potential translation between the lines."[15] The task of the translator is then to discover this essence, this intention of the original and to recreate that spirit in the new language.

II

In undertaking a translation—or writing of any sort—one is aware of the instability of language itself, as T. S. Eliot expressed it: "Trying to learn to use words, and every attempt / is a wholly new start, and a different kind of failure" ("East Coker," *Four Quartets*). One also thinks of Robert Frost's oft-cited dictum, that poetry is what gets lost in translation. Croce claimed that the best translation of Plato's *Republic* was either a xerox copy or Kant's *Critique of Pure Reason*. In light of the above considerations, the stance of the translator of poetry must be marked simultaneously by humility and hubris.

The ambivalence of this position is not unlike that of the photographer, as Susan Sontag understands it. Translations, like photographs, re-present a reality that already exists but becomes apparent only by passing through a process of portrayal, and thus only by being filtered through an individual temperament. "Picture-taking [read: translating] is both a limitless technique for appropriating the objective world and an unavoidably solipsistic expression of the singular self."[16] Sontag goes on to discuss the nature of the alleged "equivalents," which reveal both benevolent and predatory motivations. "Photography [translation] is the paradigm of an inherently equivocal connection between self and world—its version of the ideology of realism sometimes dictating an effacement of the self in relation to the world, sometimes authorizing an aggressive relation to the world which celebrates the self. . . . An important result of the coexistence of these two ideals—assault on reality and submission to reality—is a recurrent ambivalence toward photography's *means*." Translation, when layered upon an Eliotian view of language, places its practitioner, like Sontag's photographer, in a perpetual state of skepticism that "keeps oscillating between simplicity and irony."

An initial process of *selection* is intimately intertwined with—indeed, presupposed by—translation. Selection entails a prior choice of lingustic-cultural milieu, of time period, of specifically which poet and then which poem(s) the translator is drawn to of whatever style, theme, or form of expression. Selection also entails such pragmatic considerations as "translatable," further, "translatable by me," the translator, for the sensibilities of the late twentieth century. Selection is made on the level of each poem as a discrete entity, complete in itself; different poems created by the same poet must not necessarily, but often do show affinities with one another, as various manifestations of the unified source of origin. For each poet and poem the various aspects discussed theoretically above assume different form and value; thus an anthology means multiplication of those constraints and possibilities as many times over as there are poets and poems represented. It is clear that the condition described ideally as "metempsychosis" necessarily entails pragmatic compromises when attempted on any larger scale such as an anthology.

Whereas selection and translation are aspects of one and the same process, poetry and history are obviously separate entities, and a history of poetry (including a historical anthology) entails questions of historicity and of poeticality. An anthology that claims to be a "historical anthology," that is, representative of a given place over a given period of time, includes considerations of historical representativeness, a category that may, but often does not, overlap with aesthetic value, thus requiring compromises of another sort. A particular time period might elevate "innovation" as the sine qua non of good art, whereas another may choose to emphasize the value of continuity through temporality. Time itself resolves the problem—so claim our literary historians—by filtering out the works of lasting value and thus establishing a canon. But we do not yet have that kind of perspective on recent history, and "relevance" for our own time may include extra-literary concerns such as those of a political, social, and economic nature, which, of course, change with changing times.

Indeed, the translation boom of the 1960s and 1970s had to do in part with the emergence from the dull isolationism of the 1950s, as well as the shift in world powers and the rise of the Third World. New poetic voices were heard from Latin America, the Middle East, and Eastern Europe—new because of changes within the sociopolitical structures of those countries, and even newer to the Western world because they had not been translated in recent decades. Further, such literature has an ultimately viable subject matter, often depicting concrete situations in which human lives are at stake; and the tension of the poem is exponentially raised in juxtaposition to the apparent chaos of real-world events. This is not to question the aesthetic value of such poetry, for often great human feats are performed under conditions of physical duress; but neither does it guarantee its lasting value, for the urgency of the moment may occlude aesthetic formation.

Western European languages and cultures appear less remote to the United States and are generally also more similar to one another; yet this does not preclude a high degree of diversity. Modern Austria is often lumped together with West Germany, as well as with other German-speaking countries, for they share a common language and some aspects of culture and civilization. Austria, however, has a very different tradition from that of its big neighbor, differences still operative in the present age and manifest as undercurrents in the poetry being written today. After nearly half a century of upheaval and war in Central Europe, Austria is at present a relatively "quiet" country, maintaining a position of Western-style neutrality. The past three decades have been highly productive in the arts—certainly in music, and also in the literary arts. Until only recently, it was poetry and other "short forms" that constituted the dominant mode of response to the past and new beginnings for the future.

Although most of the writers live in Vienna, American audiences will look in vain for a focus on the city as an approach to modernism; analogues to Ashbery's or Hollander's poems about New York or their well-known predecessors in London and Paris simply do not exist. Reasons are numerous, but a few preliminary suggestions may be ventured. Historically and culturally, Vienna has always been the cosmopolitan center, absorbing diverse immigrants and dealing with the nation's neighbors on all sides. The sense of history is monumental, not as a feeling of a lost paradise, but as a counter-image to modernism. Thus, on the one hand, Vienna today may be viewed as a viable anachronism. On the other hand, there is an archaistic futurism that attempts to de-historicize the present in order to break both the diachronic chain and the synchronic context. Urbanization leads to a decay of central reference, as the cathedral no longer functions as the center of the city. This atomization expresses itself in poetry as fractured syntax, loss of causal connections, and multiplicity of meaning. Modern art has largely severed its connections to communal experience, instituting its own rules under which it must validate itself. Ideas travel faster than social developments; and while Austria looks to the past historically, artistically it is moving forward with increasing awareness of its own inventive activity.

The present anthology contains over 350 poems by more than fifty poets. Its time span is 1945, the "zero point" after the war, to the present; and its spatial borders are those of Austria, defined by its present political boundaries but even more by an orientation, a "mind set." With a notable opening exception, the poets were born in the twentieth century and they published after 1945—that is, primarily or exclusively in the postwar period. All the poets (again with one exception) have at least one published volume of poetry to their credit. This criterion unfortunately excluded many younger poets who are beginning to publish, primarily in journals; the magnitude of that enterprise, however, is limitless, and it thus seemed advisable to await their poetic development. The American poet Rexroth has broached the question of whether a given audience can assimilate enough of the original to justify translation.[17] Would even the ultimate translation achieve a significant resemblance? How much does Proust mean to a Chinese farmer, for example, and vice versa? Contemporary Austrian poetry, I am convinced, has a unique contribution to make to the world. Both its nearness to and its distance from an English-speaking audience justify the present undertaking. It was the power of the poetry itself that provided the motivation for selection and translation, despite the numerous occupational handicaps noted above.

I would like to thank Dr. Wolfgang Kraus and others of the *Österreichische Gesellschaft für Literatur* in Vienna for their kind cooperation and generous support of the project. Mrs. Seidlhofer at the Austrian Institute in New York has been very helpful. I am grateful also to the University of Virginia and Columbia University. I would personally like to thank Martin Green and Peter Filkins for reading the anthology in manuscript and offering many helpful suggestions. Special appreciation goes to the Austrian poets themselves, many of whom read and assisted with the translations, and all of whom were cooperative with the undertaking. It is my conviction that *they* have something to say to an audience larger than speakers of German. It is hoped that the spirit of the poem shines through in the translation as inevitably as it does in the original, enriching readers on both sides of the Atlantic.

Notes

1. Williard V. Quine, *Word and Object* (Cambridge: MIT Press, 1960); by the same author, *Ontological Relativity* (New York: Columbia University Press, 1969). Walter Benjamin, "Die Aufgabe des Übersetzers," Preface to his translation of Baudelaire's "Tableaux parisiens"; translated by Harry Zohn as "The Task of the Translator," *Illuminations*, by Walter Benjamin, ed. Hannah Arendt (New York: Harcourt, Brace & World, 1968), pp. 69–82; see also "On Language as Such and on the Language of Man," *One-Way Street and Other Writings*, by Walter Benjamin, trans. Edmund Jephcott and Kingsley Shorter (New York: Harcourt Brace Jovanovich, 1979), pp. 107–23. Jacques Derrida, *Marges de la philosophie* (Paris: Les Éditions de Minuit, 1972). See also F. Guenthner and M. Guenthner-Reutter, eds., *Meaning and Translation: Philosophical and Linguistic Approaches* (New York: New York University Press, 1978); Lillebill Grähs, Gustav Korlén, and Bertil Malmberg, eds., *Theory and Practice of Translation*, Nobel Symposium 39, Stockholm, Sept. 6–10, 1976 (Bern: Peter Lang, 1978).

2. Jorge Luis Borges, "Las versiones homéricas," in *Discusión* (Buenos Aires: Emecé, 1966); quoted by Alfred J. MacAdam, "Translation as Metaphor," *MLN* 90 (1975): 749.

3. Ezra Pound, "Cavalcanti" (1934); rpt. in *Literary Essays* (Norfolk, Conn.: New Directions, 1954), p. 200. See also T. S. Eliot's introduction to Pound's *Selected Poems* (1928); rpt. in *Ezra Pound: A Critical Anthology*, ed. J. P. Sullivan (Middlesex, England: Penguin, 1970), pp. 101–9.

4. Roman Jakobson, "On Linguistic Aspects of Translation," in *On Translation*, ed. Reuben A. Brower (New York: Oxford University Press, 1966), p. 235. Burckhardt writes: "Poetry is the least translatable of all modes of discourse, not because the poet surrounds his work with a vague aura of rich connotation, but because he treats *all* the features of the language—its rhythms, sounds, and puns, as well as the concrete meanings buried in its abstractions—as metaphors." Sigurd Burckhardt, *The Drama of Language* (Baltimore: The Johns Hopkins Press, 1970), p. 4.

5. Robert de Beaugrande, *Factors in a Theory of Poetic Translating* (Assen, The Netherlands: Van Gorcum, 1978), p. 94. The systematization and formalization of thought are newer than the ideas themselves, which have been around for centuries, but usually in the form of essayistic commentary. See *The Craft and Context of Translation: A Critical Symposium*, ed. William Arrowsmith and Roger Shattuck (Garden City, N.Y.: Anchor Books, 1964); see also Frederic Will, *The Knife in the Stone* (The Hague: Mouton, 1973).

6. Northrop Frye, *The Anatomy of Criticism* (Princeton: Princeton University Press, 1971), p. 77.

7. Ulrich von Wilamowitz-Möllendorff, "Was ist Übersetzen?" Preface to *Euripides Hippolytus, griechisch und deutsch,* trans. Wilamowitz (Berlin: Weidmann, 1892); rpt. as "Die Kunst der Übersetzung" (1924); rpt. in his *Kleine Schriften* (Berlin: Akademie-Verlag, 1972), VI, 157.

8. George Steiner, *After Babel* (Oxford: Oxford University Press, 1975), p. 359. Steiner presents a discussion of Shakespeare translations on pp. 380–92 and passim.

9. Quoted by C. Day Lewis, *On Translating Poetry* (Abington-on-Thames: Abbey Press, 1970), p. 5. Day Lewis, as poet and translator in his own right, offers interesting insights into the process.

10. Hermann Broch, "Einige Bemerkungen zur Philosophie und Technik des Übersetzens," in *Schriften zur Literatur*, Vol. IX/2 of *Kommentierte Werkausgabe*, ed. Paul Michael Lützeler (Frankfurt: Suhrkamp, 1975), 74.

11. Willis Barnstone, "ABC's of Translation," *Translation Review* 2 (Fall 1978): 35 (italics mine); see also Keith Bosley, "Fit Only for Barbarians: The Sound of Translated Poetry," *World Literature Today* 55 (Winter 1981): 52–55.

12. Ben Belitt, *Adam's Dream* (New York: Grove Press, 1978), p. 46.

13. Eugene A. Nida, *Toward a Science of Translating* (Leiden: Brill, 1964). Nida's initial work during the 1940s reflects his training in descriptive linguistics; since then he has published extensively, his most recent book being *Language Structure and Translation* (Stanford: Stanford University Press, 1975). Jiří Levý, *Die literarische Übersetzung: Theorie einer Kunstgattung* (Frankfurt: Athenäum, 1969). Levý's work reflects the influence of Russian Formalism and Prague School Structuralism, and his book includes a bibliography of Soviet and East European work on translation.

14. William Gass, "Ein Gott vermags," *American Poetry Review*, vol. 7, no. 2 (March–April 1978), 5–10.

15. Benjamin, "The Task of the Translator," p. 82.

16. Susan Sontag, *On Photography* (New York: Dell Publishing Co., Delta Book, 1977), pp. 122–26.

17. Kenneth Rexroth, "The Poet as Translator," in *The Craft and Context of Translation*, p. 23.

*Contemporary
Austrian Poetry*

RUDOLF HENZ

Rudolf Henz (1897–   ) is the oldest poet represented in this anthology and the only one born before the turn of the century—a century marked by two world wars and unheard-of human disaster. Creditably enough, Henz is still writing and publishing, as recently as *Kleine Apokalypse* in 1977 (Graz: Verlag Styria). Meanwhile he has led an active life devoted to cultural and literary activities—as reflected upon in his "Meditation at Seventy." Selections here are from the literary journal *Podium* (1971) and the anthology *Zeit und Ewigkeit* (Düsseldorf: claassen verlag, 1978).

Once Again

Once again
on an evening late in summer
sitting in my backyard,
the world-apple in my hand.
And my hand does not tremble.

Podium

Meditation at Seventy

What have I accomplished?
Constructed new gods,

described, praised them—
useful gods for the present?
Did I topple statues from their pedestal,
sing the baritone solo
at the great burial of God?
Shoot a single rocket-word into the air,
scorn foolish people privately,
but in public,
tear a single word from its root?
Did I dance on all fours
and bark,
shoot at a bank messenger,
write the story of my life in prison
as sensational reportage?
I didn't even deal in drugs.
I have done nothing, nothing
that would shake my contemporaries,
that they would find singular.

Only book after book,
line after line,
for five decades.
I have not prevented a single bomb,
not even a pistol shot,
or the lie outside my window.
Did I save a starving child in Benares,
make the kid across the street happy with a ball?
Did I object to
a Brazilian bishop because he
wouldn't give up an acre of ground?
Rescue an innocent person,
turn a thief in to court?
But to touch a heart,
somewhere in the world,
only externally,
only gently,
like the night wind from the sea,
like the sudden feeling,
of being human.

Zeit und Ewigkeit

WILHELM SZABO

Wilhelm Szabo (1901–   ) is perhaps the last living representative of a tradition of "village and farm" poetry. Highly autobiographical, his work deals with the hardships and joys of country life in northeastern Austria near the present-day Czech border. The apparent simplicity and naïveté of subject matter are often expressed in the rhyme and rhythm of folk verse by this "born poet"—who is still writing. Selections are from *Landnacht* (Wien: Jugend und Volk, 1965) and *Podium* (1971).

Untranslatable

Untranslatable
remains the rustling of the wind
among the decapitated poppies,
and the brooding of the swamp
defies expression,
the soundless slumber of desolation.
Poet, translator of silence,
now and then you cunningly
wring a word from the muteness,
a dark, uninterpretable word,
but behind it remains firm,
strange and unyielding
the Inexpressible,
accessible to no
speech.

Landnacht

Resignation

Here is the key to the writing desk
and here the one to the cabinet with the files.
In the folder there
lie the copies,
in the other one
the originals and the forms.
This for the information of my successors:
The reports are complete,
the statistics up-to-date.
If one should perchance
somewhere between the pages
find my used-up
shrunken life,
throw it
in the wastepaper basket.

Landnacht

During the Day He Held a Low-level Position

During the day he held a low-level position,
as clerk perhaps or as teacher,
unobtrusive in speech and behavior
and offensive to none of his neighbors.

At night however he broke loose
in the woods of proscribed books,
creature transformed, a werewolf,
immersed himself avidly in learning,
read—when others were possessed by cards—
secretly about man's alienation.

When he returned in the morning
to the trusted commonplace,
seemingly harmless and unsuspicious,
there sometimes gleamed
in his more knowledgeable gaze
a strange, penetrating light.

Landnacht

Threshing Machine

A giant rages in the field,
a monster made of steel.
The kernels are his daily crumbs,
the ripened grain his meal.

He slowly chews the meadows bare,
the sun burns dry and raw
and heaps its trace in rhythmic step:
the bales of deadened straw.

The fields, before they're cleared and filled
with sheaves, must bow to him.
A giant rages in the field,
a monstrous, steely whim.

Landnacht

See, it begins to come down

See, it begins to come down
so lovingly from the sky.
Is it snow again from last winter?
And you don't remember its dye!

Last time it scratched your cheek,
then disappeared without trace.
As stranger it comes again
offering a tender caress.

Soon it will change into hail,
thus it ranted and raved before.
It's snow again from last winter?
It remembers us no more!

Landnacht

"Don't Trust Anyone over Thirty!"

They don't trust
anyone over thirty

and especially not me
who was already alive
when their grandmothers
were confirmed.
They think
that I respected that Corporal
and denied
or repressed
the existence of Auschwitz,
that I'm a loner and a
member of the establishment.
I, of course,
enjoy their mistrust
and silently join them
in their opposition
to the weakness in me,
the conformist
and coward.
I wish I were young,
one of them.
I don't object
to their torn
jackets and jeans
or their beards
and long hair.
I love
the candor,
the anger, and
the sadness
in their
Christ-like faces.

Podium

[Translator's note: The title of the original is in English.]

ERNST SCHÖNWIESE

Ernst Schönwiese (1905–   ) has been active in literary affairs throughout his life, serving as journal editor, former president of the Austrian PEN club, and present program director for the Austrian radio. His poetry, which has appeared in eleven volumes, is characterized by a meditative stance with metaphysical concerns, as demonstrated by the selections from *Geheimnisvolles Ballspiel* (1964) and *Baum und Träne* (1962), both at Wiesbaden: Limes, and from *Podium* (1980).

Everything is only an image
in a mirror
that reflects another mirror.
Reflection behind reflection
ad infinitum.

Everything is only a dream
in a dream
in which you dream
that you're dreaming.

Until death shatters the mirror
and awakens the dreamer.

Geheimnisvolles Ballspiel

A bird that fell out of the nest
dreams of flying.

Until gripped by despair:
wasn't the fall the flight?

But before the wildcat eats him
he is certain
that there is no such thing
as flying.

Baum und Träne

Secret Ballgame

Throw away your old ball!
Cast off everything you have—
and yourself too!

Already the world,
a golden orb,
rolls into your lap.

Geheimnisvolles Ballspiel

Forget everything you have seen,
everything you have thought.
Exist only as ear
and hear
what the inaudible says to you.

Podium

If they really lived,
they wouldn't have to understand.
But they don't really live,
thus they always want to know.

Life
is the answer to something
that should never be asked.

Podium

ERIKA MITTERER

Erika Mitterer (1906–   ) is perhaps most well-remembered for her youthful correspondence with Rainer Maria Rilke, which began in 1924 and continued until the older poet's death in 1926. The letters exchanged were written exclusively in verse, as represented by two of the selections below. Whereas the original poems display rhyme, meter, and the highly stylized conventions characteristic of the late Rilke, the language here has been somewhat naturalized. The entire correspondence was published posthumously under the authorship of Rilke and entitled *Briefwechsel in Gedichten mit Erika Mitterer* (Wiesbaden: Insel, 1950). Mitterer has continued to write throughout her life, but she was rarely able to achieve the freshness and imaginative power of her youthful work. Further selections are from *Klopfsignale* (Wien: Jugend und Volk, 1970) and *Entsühnung des Kain* (Einsiedeln: Johannes, 1974).

Third Letter

Tell me, is it right if I stop being afraid
of knowing that my fate is bound up with yours?
Forgive the weakness! But I have long been afraid
and now I see my circle closing.

Is it too much, perhaps also too oppressive
for your dignity if one trusts you so?
You have perhaps already gone away, while
my eye still sees you in the old place.

Rarely and darkly a sense of it dawns,
then I feel it's more than I can bear;
I must speed the course of events
and tell of your greatness everywhere.

I don't understand: what possessed you
to give me, an unknown entity, a place next to you?
You are an ocean. I dreamed once for a moment
that I was the crest of your wave.

———————

Let me be the incense in your cathedral,
let me be the frame to your picture,
let me be the path. You are the goal, Rome,
that fulfills itself on its seven hills.

You are the stillness, I am the sound
that heightens its creative silence.
You are the thunder, I the terror of animals
when the storm blows round their sheds.

June 25 and 26, 1924

Briefwechsel in Gedichten mit Erika Mitterer

Seventh Answer

for Erika

I

You "white oneness," I don't want to divide you
into that which resists and that which calls;
let all colors be within you,
gradated, each to its essence.

You, the embodiment of your seven colors,
should perceive what the abundance promises;
and when it seems confusing, exceed it
ever anew with your white light.

II

It can well reach *a far-off goal,*
the gaze that ascends from our deepest selves;
somewhere a star is always inclining toward it:
thus it can reach *a far-off goal.*

Does it seem to us that each sign shakes
in a heaven that is always silent?
Shining down on our hesitation,
it attempts to match our gaze.

III

You, whose fragrance is to me
as sweet as the linden:
in greeting you once again
do I hope to bind you?

Do I intend, with my greeting,
to set you free? . . .
Dream it only, or do it:
both mean *to be.*

July 28 and 29, 1924

Briefwechsel in Gedichten mit Erika Mitterer
[by Rainer Maria Rilke]

The Lord

He was so handsome and gracious, and also a good swimmer.
And he told her about the big hunt.
He invited her to the bar and laid, slightly embarrassed,
a very thick book on the wobbly table.
In it were many fish and only a bit of text,
and he was English. For he was
a Lord from England. And so touchingly shy
for twenty-eight years! She liked him.
Such a pleasant pastime was new.
She thought: A hunt—? and the forest! I could ride . . .
And dogs. And. . .perhaps. . .a child? No, six!
They would have it good! We would always have money.
"How beautiful, the blue fish with red fins!"
"You like it?" "It's fascinating!"

"Most women don't like fish."
"I'm not like most women!" "No,
you're not. . . ." He brought her home.
He kissed long and lovingly. Not like a Lord.
The next evening they met again.
Looked at the second volume of fish,
only gently touching, as if by chance,
their knees under the table. Then he asked,
not raising his voice—it's not important
and really doesn't play a role . . . but
he would like to know—"How many lovers—
you call them Schätzli?—Whatever, how many
have you had (pardon my asking!)?"
She answered in one breath
without even pausing—
"Well. . . ten. . . casually.—I like this fish."
It darted away in the flood of her tears
that no one saw.—Why did I lie?
"Oh, ten indeed?" He was not badly shaken.
"What did you expect?—I must go now,
I'm cold." "But we did not finish
our book. . . May I give it to you?"
"No thanks. Goodbye."
O forest, o hunt, o horse, dogs. . . children?
That's over. Goodbye forever!

Klopfsignale

"Dialogue"

I ask:
How much is five
times five?
I probably
miscalculated
(since they kept talking)
and I distrust
finished results. . .

And you reply:
Blue, with silver bands.

That's indisputable.

Klopfsignale

Departure

How good to leave everything!
Always ready. . .
But the secure room
with the comforting books?
But the bed, that haven
in dreamless sleep?
But the linden tree
now before blossom time?
Its smell awakens
the heart's expectations. . .
The children, full of future:
All possibilities,
all defeats,
all triumphs of love. . .

No, spring is
unsuitable for farewell.
Let me stay a bit longer!
Until the turn of summer.
Or—until the November rain. . . ?
But will I then want to give up the fire
and step out into the watery night?

To leave This and That
is overwhelmingly difficult.
To leave everything is easy.
Call me! I'll not look back. . .

Entsühnung des Kain

Portrait of an Old Man

That hopes are never fulfilled
he bore with composure, as if
it were a blessing to have had them,
glowing goldenly in the dreary day.

That wishes remain open, like the
jaws of skin-colored orchids
that seek insects in the greenhouse,
he was accustomed to it.

But as he noticed one day that the wishes
had tenderly wilted without hope's moisture,

that they had shriveled up, curled at last
soft and small round the stem, he screamed angrily:

But God, something has to remain!
At least despair! But since he
did not hope any more neither did he despair
but was content and happy like a garden dwarf.

Klopfsignale

ROSE AUSLÄNDER

Rose Ausländer (1907–   ) was born of German-Jewish parentage in the Ukrainian city of Chernovtsy. With Paul Celan she shares not only birthplace but also the fate of the "homeless" Jewish poet, persecuted and forced to leave her homeland. She lived in New York from 1946 to 1963 before returning to Germany, where she currently resides in Düsseldorf. Her poetry, which is similar to Celan's in both theme and form, appeared in nine volumes in the 1960s and 1970s and has been collected in *Gesammelte Gedichte* (Köln: Braun, 1977).

Cézanne

From him rocks
and trees learned
to be transparent

Hills
of ether
irrevocable

Green essence
green
in blue skin

The outline
the inner intensity:
matter without mass

Gesammelte Gedichte

In the Chagall Village

Slanting gables
hang on the
horizon

The fountain sleeps
lighted by
cat eyes

The peasant woman
milks the goat
in the dream stall

Blue
the cherry tree on the roof
where the bearded old man
plays the violin

The bride
gazes into the eye of the flower
hovers on the veil
above the night steppe

In the Chagall village
the cow grazes
on the moon meadow
golden wolves
protect the lambs

Gesammelte Gedichte

Still Life

Chrysanthemums
in the coffin-vase
Quiet dying
exhaled in decay

The water in the glass
sleeps
its innumerable eyes
blind

On the skin of the grapes
taut in death

the sun paints
the sheen of breath

Only the clock
is alive
its lips
drink the time.

Gesammelte Gedichte

Evening

Shadows steal
past the window
thieves
with stolen hours
in their arms

your stolen time

You lean
out the window
test the cool air
the distance from the first star
to you
a handspan
from here to there

The thieves
are putting their heads together

Gesammelte Gedichte

Sunday on Riverside Drive

Landscape white-washed by water The wind
plays its game with the clouds Sea-gulls are oval
Movement around a long knife A ship that
cuts the Hudson without wounding it
 The world rages blackly from the leafless newspaper

Elegance oils the promenade Children on roller skates fly

into the light Even August becomes green behind park benches
along the unbroken parade of cars
        The world rages blackly from the leafless newspaper

The sun accompanies the white metal wagon of the
ice cream vendor who is hoarse from calling his
two syllables On the other side of the river on higher
terrain August is green around sober houses A few
ships sleep in the harbor Higher up in thick mist
the Washington Bridge hangs dream-like real
        The world rages blackly from the leafless newspaper

We bring Sunday to Riverside Drive We
throw the car-clamor into the water We
throw the weight of the week into the water We
throw the world into the water so it can wash itself clean
        of coal and ash.

Gesammelte Gedichte

Romeo and Juliet in Central Park

Romeo and Juliet
in Central Park
don't tell their parents
on the other end of the earth
where the weeping willow
NO
weeps

Juliet and Romeo
two green fires
in the grass
embarrassed by
June air
heart-here

Dance of the cars
chipmunk eyes and the
merry-go-round
in rotation

Past the dollar faces
fly
breath-like clouds
June smell

the green globe
in ring-flower play

Romeo and Juliet
deathless
under the aspen
red lightning on their eyelids
green sun in their ear
Romeo-lips
Juliet-hair
the globe circles
around the green YES
around the red YES
around breathless grass

Gesammelte Gedichte

Harlem at Night

He draws the long threads
from the trumpet
winds them
around Harlem's
jungle

Soft ribbons roll
from his African eyes
sadness

Mushroom rockets
shoot into the
black heaven

above the blues

Only an echo
reels in the distance
before the soul
expires

Gesammelte Gedichte

ALFRED GESSWEIN

Alfred Gesswein (1911–83) was both poet and visual artist, as evidenced by the pictorial metaphors and spatial forms in the selections from *Vermessenes Gebiet* (Salzburg: O. Müller, 1967), *Zielpunkt* (Baden: Grasl, 1977), and *Beton wächst schneller als Gras* (München: Delp, 1977). Until his recent death he served as editor of the literary journal *Podium* and as co-editor of the poetry series *Lyrik aus Österreich*.

Watteau's Coloration

Watteau's color:
atmospheric May

Musical motives
of a blackbird
embroidered on the trees

Lovers
now find words
that bloom on bushes
only a wind is needed
to make them soar
a flock of white doves

The lake decides
to be blue like the sky

No one notices
the dying of the hour

Vermessenes Gebiet

the days count again

the sky
gains
in significance
one sits
on his
five letters
in the sun
drinks air
out of march cups
the yellow
beaks of the
children are wide
open

the sea gulls
carouse
in travel fever
the fish watch
for anglers
in front of sold-out
places in the sun
a parade passes by
baby carriages
and walking sticks

Zielpunkte

possible landscape

the foreground
dominated by
marten and fox in front of
a deserted farm

the sky
corresponding to the season
a flock of wild ducks
or crows

diagonally
across the landscape
an irregular line of willows:
the stream

in the distance
patches of land
on the horizon
ascending green
or painted rust-brown
or wintry:
the snow compressed

essential
is the path above
the horizon
with the
invisible
goal

Zielpunkte

Landscape of a Face

Unexplainable
the perpetual attempt
to retrace
the lines of a face
not yet overcome
by events
war
prosperity
resignation
still unaltered
the ocular of the eyes

Landscape
with a horizon
only suggested
narrow roads
that end in a thicket

Familiarity
strangeness in the face
that you perhaps
see through
at an encounter
in a streetcar
around a house corner

or in the letters
on a billboard

Contours
that trickle away
sand in the sandbox

Unexplainable
the perpetual attempt
to retrace the lines
of a face
that once perhaps
was yours

Beton wächst schneller als Gras

Sometimes
only in the reflection of
a store window
I notice
changes in myself
depression weighs
more heavily than cement
my shoulders hang
and already there is some
regression with the
awful dread
of going down
often my feet
don't rise so quickly
from the tallow candle
to the robot brain
beside the bulldozers
and airhammers
who can hear
his own heart

it gets colder
concrete grows
faster than grass

Beton wächst schneller als Gras

JULIANE WINDHAGER

Juliane Windhager (1912–   ) continues her lifelong writing career, as evidenced by her recent volume, *Schnee-Erwartung* (Salzburg: Residenz, 1979). She often fuses nature, as the principal poetic theme, with personal experience and childhood memories.

St. Nicholas

The nave of the church
foretells gray, gray
down into the ground
with the tower
and the knowing brows
in the choir windows.

On the coastline
only a faint contour
is visible.

Here
Columbus knelt
on the day
of departure
here he invoked
and entreated the
sea star.

During the cold
centuries

bat wings
have grown
on the angels.

Schnee-Erwartung

Confirmation Day

As they were
having coffee
fourteen people
with porcelain
cups and fine silver

and the white
cousin came into the room
suddenly grown-up

and the classical house
across the street
drowned in
watery sunlight

there was nothing
static any more
in the relations.
Someone got up
and closed
the curtains.

Schnee-Erwartung

Fata Morgana

The street belongs
to the noontide witch
in the high summer
of the white Baba.

She crosses
our path
she casts
her spell:

Sand becomes wave
wheels will plough
through the water
water is not wet
Sand becomes sand.

Schnee-Erwartung

Children's Carnival

My jumping jack
his green leg
his red leg
buried
since summer
under the sand
of the playground.

There the snow
forms a nice cover
only his green-red cap
grows
and grows
it slides down
on my forehead
there the balloons
are already wrinkled.

One can't always
be merry
the room—warm
from the round—
is no longer clear.

My jumping jack
grins in the mirror.
I can no longer eat
green-red ice cream.

Schnee-Erwartung

CHRISTINE BUSTA

Christine Busta (1915–   ) achieves a type of "modern classicism," as representative of the tradition of Austrian poetry. Her works, which have consistently met with wide popular success, include the following: *Lampe und Delphin* (1955), *Die Scheune der Vögel* (1958), *Unterwegs zu älteren Feuern* (1965), *Salzgärten* (1975), and *Wenn du das Wappen der Liebe malst* (1981), all at Salzburg: O. Müller.

Life on this Star

Where can one live? We inherited sidereal cities:
the stairs unusable, the rooms inhuman, inhabited by day
by the sun, that fearless lioness, and at night the
estranged windows besieged by darkness and stars.

Nestlings of the earth. For a while we were tolerated.
Now we are outcasts, fledged like rain and snow, and we
nest through the winter in the terrible walls of the wind.

Lampe und Delphin

The Angel with the Sun Dial
(Cathedral at Chartres)

He divides the hours into casts of the shadow,
the measure of light is shield for his heart,
for who can fathom the darkness?
Each day is crucified on his chest.
His face shows time indivisible.

Unterwegs zu älteren Feuern

Poems

Life,
preserved in amber,
buried.

Scars,
touchable,
inviolable.

Recorded time
coming to be.
Chalk or agate.

Salzgärten

Salt Gardens

Above dried-up
river beds
the phoenix flower
blooms invisibly
out of the white
ashes of the sea.

Salzgärten

An Olive Tree in Corfu

In Corfu (I was not there)
a friend once bought for me,
without sign and seal,
only on good faith,
an olive tree.
It stands on the shore of a bay
and has since become my most prized possession,
mine like nothing else
because I make no demands.

I cannot care for it,
will never in my life see it,
but it is there.
I know it looks after the ships,
gives lodging to wind and light,
and with my smooth olives
it entertains strangers.
To no one need I refuse its shadow,
I can without worry
grant hospice to anyone,
and my treeless and sealess window
is by day and by night
full of departure and arrival.

My olive tree becomes more beautiful each year.
Secretly I am already looking for
an heir to it.
One needs no testament
to obtain my Corfu.

Salzgärten

The Prodigal Son

You need not kill the calf for me, a bowl of soup will do.
But let me eat it outside on your doorstep,
inside everything is too secure and confined for a homesickness
    like mine,
and I can't get far enough away from it.
It continually sends me out and then everything throws me
    back again. Here I am.
Don't ask how faithlessly one who is lost to fidelity loses
    himself.

Ask me about the wind, the snow, the rivers and stars,
about the beggars in the country, the barns, hailed-out
   harvests,
grapes, husks, and words between the stones in the fire,
about the butterfly in the sand, the smell of dried-up wells.
Empty out my knapsack, it's overflowing with abandoned
   treasures.
A bird skin is among them and a bottle-message,
which even the salt does not extinguish.
I need no answer, no inheritance,
plow your grayest poppy field for me
and fill me forever with sleep.

Salzgärten

Raymondsville

Hidden entrance to an overgrown path.
No servant beckons, only red berry bushes,
the guests are not announced here.

They come like dreams in the sleep
of genius and ghosts, people enclosed
in a white house on the slope densely green.

The gray stairway doors open
to those who wish to rest
at a bench on the terrace above
by a round table, served nothing
but sound through the silent wall.

In front, the garden, a stage for the rain,
mountains like dark smoke in the fog silver,
stage-sets, continually pushed gently back,
time in the grass, fate in the trees,
life again, earth, water, air.

Salzgärten

Anatolia

There the sea spoke to us
for many nights with harsh words,
but the fishing huts were nests full of sleep
and we drank stars
out of the cisterns.

The farmer was poor, oppressed
but the fruit he offered the guest
shone with gladness.
Shining too were the eyes of the son
who sprang from the dry womb of the earth
to the heart of the stranger
and recognized him as father
without the guilt of conception.

There we climbed up the steps
to the disowned gods
and measured loss and sadness
on broken ashlar
while the heavens in wake
of the scene that became empty
descended forever.

Salzgärten

Experiences

Of all the things lost there is one
I would like to have back:
the simple-framed slate board

on which I learned to write so carefully
since the slate pens broke easily,
on which the signs vanished so quickly

that I feared for *ov* and *v*

on which I had to erase *Monnur* and *Mniui*

eager for new words,
sad because they also passed,

until suddenly—confounded and comforted—
I discovered the scratched traces in bare black,
they all remained there as cipher.

Salzgärten

Under a Reading Lamp

The finely-spun threads of the script
with which we sewed our lives together,
the artful patterns in books, in letters,
cut them open again line by line.

Tie together the *spoken* language
from man to man and speak through being,
like the patient objects do.

Transform all paper back into
the secret of the old forest
and compress the self into tree rings,
the original cosmic script for illiterates.

Salzgärten

MAX HÖLZER

Max Hölzer (1915–   ) has much in common with Paul Celan, including their friendship in Paris. Like Celan, he began in the tradition of surrealism and developed toward a hermeticism in which the poem questions its own efficacy, as in *Nigredo* (Frankfurt: Insel, 1962). Unlike Celan, his later work expresses a turn to the "here" rather than the "there," with an attendantly stronger realistic element, as exemplified in *Gesicht ohne Gesicht* (Frankfurt: Fischer, 1968), from which the present selections are largely taken. The title of his most recent volume, *Mare occidentis. Das verborgene Licht. Chrysopöe* (Pfullingen: Neske, 1976) indicates his interest in the symbolic, alchemistic potential of language.

Mysterious Geometry

Mysterious geometry of the morning.
The empty streets keep the place awake.
Each curve of the wall lives by its form,
each flight of the dove.

The gray is pure, as if man didn't exist.
The houses don't seem to be built in his image.
A memory, devoid of content,
has returned.
Without thinking, I will soon be home.
The anticipation itself is an ocean of light.
My self has its power in the unnameable.

Weren't my thoughts and words
like the tumbling and driving of the evening?
All pride,
everything I had written,
every exchange of energy for intention
burned
in the ritual of the night,
of the prostitution.

Mysterious geometry of the morning . . .

Gesicht ohne Gesicht

He let the house be

He let the house be, wanted it to be without a name.
(The things, when the hour is favorable,
will shine
in a face without face . . .)

The steep curve of the street—
hostile
like an embrace that he didn't invoke.
It blows the granite-dust
up into his teeth.

His monologs in the dark, they are
not yet like the dry, pathetic
jaw-breaking
of the bats in their dance.

The wishing finally explodes—
but in the gold of a painting
it is banished by the stream of urine
that a slow brain pours out . . .

The owl does not fly out of the silence,
neither does the mountain climb out of a forest of silence.
The body is not the grave of silence.
Silence does not dig it up.

His skin is so loud that he is followed by
the house, the bed, the books,
the shadows, carried
by the spectral elephant of the word.

He derides his writing, endlessly. . . . The cold,
even the cold is a lie. Blind,
as if he had broken his face,
he stands in the morning.

Gesicht ohne Gesicht

The Summer's Cold

Not the dark café, not today; I want color,
    and the oppositions still seem too conciliable.

That coast was steep, nowhere the sea deeper, but the stillness
    of the depths broke out in hissing and thunder.

If I lose myself now in the noise, it will be like then—
    dead still. That means for a while

my collusion . . . Oh, in rage against the world

you secretly spread out your arms to embrace it. In contrast,
    the ocean: far out in the middle it rolls up the water-heart

and lets it flow out, as if it hated its own strength and not
    the constraint of the shore.

You complain that life is a trap, time a chain:

then you praise its hesitating space and its inherent
    flowing. How is one supposed to understand that?

Your word creates fear, but fear is only the desire
    for love and the haste to destroy it.

The waves, subject to no one's will, drive themselves, rear up,
    and break down. Impatiently

they dash to pieces what is washed ashore, bones, star shells,

as if there weren't an eternity to grind them small and smooth.

My poem is uncomfortable, and the sand there remains coarse,

and when the step falters and sinks down in the mire,
    one can see

how unreachable, how far out the sickle of the shore is
    stretched: with its white point it pierces through

where everything stops, into the white. Is there a place

that doesn't border on other places?—not like this café
    on the street and the people, or the street on the
    stores and houses,

in which it is at once dark and light . . . but no one
    can see me, I who am all this

and alone traverse that arch between ocean and
    dry land, without a beyond,

a dead man who glows in the southern sun, while water
    from the deep well, the summer's cold, gushes
    over my feet.

Gesicht ohne Gesicht

And the cunning of the poem, that it consumes the world. . .
Take from it the smoke screen of the good.
It belongs to the dead, the possessed (your haste
leaves nothing behind but a notch on the post).

Gray storms veil the horizon.
Arteries glow as if in embryos.
    You have received peace.
                              Death's thousand-spring
renders the recurring joy lonely.

Endless incisions of seeing . . . Your
                              wind rose
blooms.
    The fall of the ridges
                              remains far.
Scaly, a tall roof—it doesn't support the feeling.
You are a thousand pilgrims—and none of them.

    . . . Watched, withheld compassion:
    when he was blind, they took down the tree.
Steep street, the shadows, the streaks of sun,
(while you climb and become ever lighter),

burn and cool, expose the betrayal.
Clouds that blow it away.
                              The entrails,
singly, of the Son, flown from the cross, wrapped
in oxides, grasses, the script.
                              Petrified
grapes, dragging in sand, in absolute
    space.

Hard-eyed, his race, from afar,
uncovers the heart.
The brain—the defoliated
throat.
The belly, white vault, the tongue.

It leaves me
to myself and the stones.
Reveal nothing, nothing conceal.
(This day does not need the soul—it is
without exit. Its light separates heaven and cloister.)

Gesicht ohne Gesicht

Sète

Intoxicated by absence, oh no longer
in the chain of the arteries . . . A sea shines.
Hardly more lifeless than an abandoned dream—
the cubical blocks, the iron bars
of the fortress: insect at the bottom of the stone quarry.

Down to the depths of dead lives
grows the desire, clear waterfall,
the island, free from deferment.
The sun throws gray folds over itself,
the horizon is effaced like a wonder.

The mountain comes to itself up into the dust,
it opens the paths for the sinking light.
In you was the sea. Its nakedness flows
up with the air, the blue chest,
and rubs itself milkily on the rock body.

Gesicht ohne Gesicht

I accompanied the Castilian
earth like a woman who is
cold and hot.

On the border of night
she blossomed: desert of
fearlessness.

The violet
unremembered
tugged and preyed on its own senses.

Dew
multiplied the solitude (as if love
were a return to itself).

Oh air-hands
disclosed the burden of dying
behind the eyes.

I see the inclination
of its unalloyed breadth.

Gesicht ohne Gesicht

In the "Trocadero"

The earth, paved, freezes
even in the mild spring
like a trampled leg . . .

At night
you visited me, with
testingly lowered brow,
under the noontide we
sat to the table.
A small round
silence per-
haps
offered itself
undivided
to eat.
And not at all absent we
reached for the bread.

Today it stretches itself out here,
from the same table of false
ash: not
into the pictureful beyond,
but, like a name,
into the self-
less.

Salt, wagon-
tracks in the

empty
heart.

Mare occidentis. Das verborgene Licht. Chrysopöe

CHRISTINE LAVANT

Christine Lavant (1915–73) is recognized as a major poet, although her work defies all classification. Religious mysticism, nature magic, and the extremes of ecstasy and despair—at once metaphysical and existential—are characteristic of her poetry, which seemed to grow out of a personal life plagued by isolation, poverty, and illness in rural Carinthia. Major volumes include *Die Bettlerschale* (1956), *Spindel im Mond* (1959), and *Der Pfauenschrei* (1962); collected in *Kunst wie meine ist nur verstümmeltes Leben* (1981), all at Salzburg: O. Müller.

Up and down without a bridge
blows the wind across the waters,
partly dry with fever-words,
partly harsh with fever-holds.
From their sleep it tears the willows,
wholly silver-white in fear,
turns around the vine's soft tendrils,
binding them to strange, stiff branches,
hostile to the core.

Up and down upon the bridge
comes my brain out from the half-sleep,
speaking half-clear words of sorrow,
counting half-true mental pictures.
Feverishly it ploughs the fire
and surrounds the willow's fear,
disentangling twisted tendrils,

coolness and a peace as prelude
for the final fall.

Kunst wie meine . . .

In the empty center of the cyclone
safe and secure my heart looks out
on its uprooted images
and the flight of all refuge.
The house of the world has been razed;
swarms of angels descend from heaven
into the hearts of men,
there to incite terror.
I have not released my heart.
It crosses under the burning sail
through immeasurable suffering,
followed by a resolute angel
and the horror of persecution.

Kunst wie meine . . .

You have taken me away from all joy.
Yet I will suffer exactly,
and very exactly only as long
as it pleases me, Lord.
You have me in a state of
wildest pride and most savage mind.
Lift your hand and strike me down,
I shall then only spring up higher,
and you will have me before you forever,
a small, red, angry ball.
Every position throws me back to you
because you took me away from that place
where I was heart and happy and soft like a bird,
in order to roll me together
and cast me into eternal suffering.

Kunst wie meine . . .

None of the easy remedies has proved effective.
Obliquely through the lamp light
a still greater fear reaches out every evening
and says: we must journey to hell
before it strikes midnight!
My hope rests in God's sleeve.
Never yet has he noticed its presence,
it was never a burden to him.
It is good not to have it by my side
on these horrible nocturnal journeys
when I am intoxicated with pride and impotence
and always go down to just before hell.
But inebriates are not admitted.
It will be difficult to stay drunk forever,
for all remedies fail at some point.
There remains finally only despair.

Kunst wie meine . . .

When your name is added
the still, speechless signs
indicate something strange.
I have not yet received even half
of my heart back from the world;
the other half, hidden, speaks
in unintelligible sounds.
Every night your name hangs over me
on the hair of an angel, and every night
it grows a new shell,
a new secret around its core.
When will the world give me back my share,
that half of my heart which long ago
was loosened and misled?
When will I come into my strength?
For strength and experience will be needed
to shuck your name from those husks
and with it on my tongue to read the signs
between dying and death.

Kunst wie meine . . .

Through these glassy afternoons
irredeemably possessed birds
swarm toward the mountains
under the trembling sun.

Yellow unrest in every bush.
The woods with red foreheads
listen feverishly on brown hills.

A strange wind on the shore
gathers willow leaves and vines;
fearfully the bright raft
glides into the frosty black water.

No one speaks to the earth.
Under the flocks of frenzied birds
it speechlessly comprehends the evening.

Kunst wie meine . . .

I asked the headless snake
and dipped my hands in the moon-blood;
now I go to heal the unlucky star
so that it can ascend again
before my hands betray it.
The hill lifts me up a bit,
in the moon-blood I see the mirror of the sea;
there the star cowers in a coral reef
and calls for help like a bird.
Not for the first time do I hear the call,
my breath has cut it off many times before,
has beheaded the snake and quartered the moon,
all in search of your name.
It however avoids injury;
only after ascension can it be retrieved,
only my lucky star can bring it back
and put it in the round moon
and place it on the tail of the snake
and my heart in the reef of the coral.

Kunst wie meine . . .

For you I have exchanged the lights
and increased by one the points of the compass;
my breath, which laboriously goes through my bones,
outripens the flower of my heart and swells
its semen in the sense of your rose.
A steel band holds the loose root
of my tongue in check and places
your name as an eye in nine cortices.
Soon you will find in you a tree of blessing,
a thorn above thorns which, to prevent wholeness,
harms everything that could heal you.
In my larynx—constellation that is chokingly silent—
I lift the lights, one of which rises
to lessen the force of your pain.

Kunst wie meine . . .

Slyly the sadness trickles down
into the caverns of secret joy.
Yet I must go down to the depths!
Even if I drown nine times
I must retrieve your image from the water
before it is saltily petrified.
It is no longer a matter of temporal joy;
turned away, I want to conceal you
in the heart of the Father.
Too much has already been drowned in me,
but you must become a wonderful flame
in the top half of the world,
while I—deeply and more deeply distressed—
feel the brand as it scars my heart.

Kunst wie meine . . .

Similar people don't hear one another.
Separated, my call now rises
from the branches that no longer shake,
and it wants—before arriving at your tree—
to achieve the hardness of silence.
Perhaps a stone will fall in you

just when you decide
to become the nest of a bird?
Similar people don't hear one another.
We have haunted each other too similarly,
but now, if I endure transformation
and come like a stone to hurt you,
your resin will pour out over me
and your listening over my silence.

Kunst wie meine . . .

JEANNIE EBNER

Jeannie Ebner (1918–   ) is a prominent figure on the Austrian literary scene and a prolific writer of novels, poems, essays, and translations, as well as former editor of the journal *Literatur und Kritik.* Her long list of publications includes *Gedichte* (Gütersloh: S. Mohn, 1965), from which the present selections are taken.

Dialogue

Where have you been?
I've been walking through torrents of water.
I've been singing.

Where have you been?
I was dead. Snow fell in my mouth.
I was silent.

Where have you been?
I drank and was drunk by others.
I lived.

I want to lay my forehead on your feet
and be tired.
You must go on.

Gedichte

98

Hunger

Your head comes like a ship with full freight.
We are waiting at the harbor. We are hungry.
You brought gold and ivory from the black coast,
but the children are hungry for milk
               and fall down like sick flowers.

We brought up our heart. It grew,
became a tree and bore fruit that never ripens:
hands that reach out into emptiness.
Whirling emptiness fills your sails with new wind
and your head, like a sun on the horizon, goes up and down,
laden with the pale fruit of our hearts.

We have buried our children
in towers of gold and ivory.
Now we are waiting again at the harbor.
And are hungry. And don't know for what.

Gedichte

On the Way

You have already put too much in my hands.

The first thing I gave away,
the second, I discarded,
the third, I bartered off,
the fourth, I lost somewhere on the way.

I don't want to take anything more.
You offer me a ring, a crown, a knife—
shall I give it away again, sell it or lose it?
I hold my hands under the sun and rain
and drink from them, and time passes.
When was all that?

Gedichte

Moment after the Rain

No, I don't believe, as they say, that I
lived more intensively as a child than today.
I don't share their idle melancholy, their plaintive lament
over a vanished, more beautiful childhood.
I don't question, like those who incessantly ask with a sigh:
Was everything so different then? Was it always springtime?

It was so: In the morning the sun shone (as always)
on the apple tree at the back,
and the grass was not fresher and greener there.
After the rain (as today) things were filled with a luster
and the smell of grass hovered in the afternoon dream
over the small place.
Children sang at the window (wind carried the fragrance into
   the room)
"The grass is wet, the grass is wet. . ." and they still sing.

Years fell like rain. My hand on the table: Look at it!
It is old and wrinkled. Nevertheless it is.
No, I don't believe that the past can be better.
The grass is wet, the grass is wet. . . How full the moment is!
Don't look back. Here all time begins to turn green with joy.
Don't you know who you are?

Gedichte

RUDOLF BAYR

Rudolf Bayr (1919–   ) was born in Linz and has lived also in Vienna and Salzburg as a free-lance writer, working at literary journals and radio stations. He is known primarily as a dramatist, but he also writes poetry, prose, and essays which display an admixture of classical Greek and Christian elements. Selections are from his volume of poetry entitled *Der Wolkenfisch* (Salzburg: Residenz, 1964), as well as from the anthology *Zeit und Ewigkeit* (Düsseldorf: claassen verlag, 1978).

The Cloud-Fish

Yellow, dandelion-yellow in the low December
the afternoon pushes the fourth hour.
Through smoke and cold the earth moves forward
under dandelion sky
breathlessly toward the long-handed evening.
In the net of branches the cloud-fish quivers.

Der Wolkenfisch

Late at Night

To write down a word late at night
which just barely rehabilitates the day;

to remember a moment late at night
which just barely rehabilitates the day;
to rehabilitate the day late at night,
just barely rehabilitate:
with a word,
a remembered moment—
probably however the day is past help
late at night,
with no moment,
no memory,
with no word;
the very early morning writes with wide chalk
on fear.
The day will rehabilitate fear.

Zeit und Ewigkeit

The Voice

The voice that summons you
is at first not even a voice,
only acoustic embryo
that penetrates the flattened indifference.
You are startled and listen and notice
a bit of fear trickles out.

A motorcycle punctuates skids in the lurking night.

You break a piece of justification from memory
to cover the spot
that perpetrated awakening.
The best antidote to morality is morality.

At the breakfast table sits the confident day.
Covered with hoarfrost around the rose rondeau
in front of the hospital to the Holy Ghost
the welfare line is en route.

Regret has found the hole in memory.
You tighten the circle; measure backwards
and put it in place;
then the same curve forwards.
How much future remains;
enough to afford deafness.

The voice that summons you:
a situation can be its mouthpiece,
a smell its arrow,
a farewell unlock its message.
It occurs as number
in the careful calculation
or falls from the newspaper,
a tiny announcement.
For it is re-trained in banalities,
removed from the altars,
and put on duty
where you can use it.

Der Wolkenfisch

MICHAEL GUTTENBRUNNER

Michael Guttenbrunner (1919–   ) incorporates the poles of Mediterranean vitality and apocalyptic demise in his poetry, which often reflects his personal experiences in the war. Selections are from *ungereimte gedichte* (1959) and other works as collected in *Gesang der Schiffe* (1980), both at Düsseldorf: claassen verlag.

The Snake Star

My beloved has already been
with me in filth and splendor.
But never like now: naked as a star at night.
The radiant one entwines me snakelike
and whispers: Come into me.
You shall be with me in paradise.

ungereimte gedichte

Metamorphosis

You soared westward above the wood,
I followed you slowly along the muddy path, and
when the moon arose I was already deep in the woods.
There I saw you in the mirror

of a death-still spring,
but you, as stream, ran away crying.

ungereimte gedichte

Reflection

Sometimes when everything had become still
and even the war held its bellowing breath
for a moment,
I heard the worms crawl in the earth
or the snow fall. And heard your feet
going softly to and fro deep in my heart
and saw myself in the mirror of your eyes
and saw my true face.

ungereimte gedichte

The Landing

The odor of thyme
blows from the mountains.
Oil vapors rot in the sun,
discarded fat from animals
slaughtered along the way.

The waves chatter feverishly
with the prows of ships and beat
the horny chest of the island.
Flanks roar, helmeted hills
clatter on the periphery.

Drunk with death-wine
the giant ships rock.
Death messengers whistle
ear-shatteringly
from the pitching galleys.

Red and black,
it lies on the shore:
shed blood,
dried-up fly food.

Under the blackish sun,
between the network of fishers
and soldiers the springs dry up,
and around the contaminated fountains
lie the drinkers.
The deadly words dissolve
in the purple sea.

Gesang der Schiffe

The Test

After the sun had sunk
over the bloodbowl
of earth
the Lord appeared.
The fallen corpses
checkered the field's
blackness like snow,
and the damp roses
of wounds shone bluely.
His cloud-covered head
appeared above me,
dripping in moonlight,
and asked if I were still able
to bear the murder.

Gesang der Schiffe

Return

Much happens in silence,
when the storm cries itself red
or the stars shine angrily.
Oh, then the street chokes
on the deaf stones,
and the scream of the step spins around,
and grief wails up through the cracks.

Don't touch it!
Suppress the terrible sound!

Return to the rose
of an earlier time,
when you, as shepherd,
called into the valley of desire,
and the sheep came to you.

Gesang der Schiffe

The Guardian Angel

In flowing garments
with wings of a swan,
for many years he stayed
protectively by the child.
But one day he led it
to an abyss,
and with holy hands
making the sign of the cross
above the curly crown,
he shoved it over the edge.

Gesang der Schiffe

Occupation

Like an animal on all fours
he sometimes crawls forth
and lies in wait
between screeching barrel-organs.
There an anguishing wheel
still turns,
and above grinding chains
hovers a whirl of dust.
He utters only a few words
like some prophetic song
and crawls back silently
into the protective darkness.

Gesang der Schiffe

Dead Poet in the Mountains

He looks up the high walls
to the peaks, which
spread their white faces
high in the blue,
and he thinks he hears bells
after the long silence
in his breast.
But he is deluded
by impotent attachment
to the large scale,
and nothing happens.

Gesang der Schiffe

PAUL CELAN

Paul Celan (1920–70) is recognized as one of the leading poets in modern literature, comparable perhaps to Rilke or Hölderlin. Born in the Ukrainian city of Chernovtsy and raised in the Chassidic tradition, he experienced the horrors of the concentration camps, a topic that finds expression also in his poetry. From 1948 until his suicide in 1970 he lived in Paris. Besides an early work, *Der Sand aus den Urnen* (Wien: A. Sexl, 1948), nine major volumes of his poetry have appeared: *Mohn und Gedächtnis* (1952) and *Von Schwelle zu Schwelle* (1955), both at Stuttgart: Deutsche Verlags-Anstalt; *Sprachgitter* (1959) and *Die Niemandsrose* (1963), both at Frankfurt: Fischer; *Atemwende* (1967), *Fadensonnen* (1968), *Lichtzwang* (1970), *Schneepart* (posthumously 1971), and *Zeitgehöft* (posthumously edited, 1976, comprising poems written mainly in 1969–70), all five at Frankfurt: Suhrkamp. The selection here includes representatives from each of the volumes, presented in chronological order and illustrating Celan's development.

Eyes:
shining with rain that poured down
when God enjoined me to drink.

Eyes:
gold that the night counted into my hands
when I gathered nettles
and rooted the shadows of sayings.

Eyes:
evening that flared up when I opened the gate

and, wintered by the ice of my temples,
burst through the towns of eternity.

Mohn und Gedächtnis

He who tears his heart out of his breast at night reaches for
   the rose.
His is its leaf and its thorn,
for him it lays the light on the plate,
for him it fills the glasses with breath,
for him the shadows of love rustle.

He who tears his heart out of his breast at night and hurls it
   high:
he does not miss the mark,
he stones the stone,
for him the blood sounds from the clock,
for him the hour knocks the time from his hand:
he is allowed to play with more beautiful spheres
and to speak of you and of me.

Mohn und Gedächtnis

Brand

We didn't sleep any longer, for we lay in the clockwork of
   sadness
and bent its hands like switches,
and they snapped back and whipped time down to its blood,
and you spoke in the falling twilight,
and twelve times I said you to the night of your words,
and it opened and stayed open,
and I laid one eye in its lap and braided the other into your
   hair
and bound the two with a fuse, the open artery—
and a new flash of lightning came down.

Mohn und Gedächtnis

The years from you to me

Again your hair waves when I cry. With the blue of your eyes
you set the table of love: a bed between summer and fall.
We drink what somebody brewed who was not I nor you nor
  a third person:
we sip on emptiness and finality.

We look at ourselves in the mirrors of deep sea and pass the
  food faster:
the night is the night, it begins with the morning,
it lays me to you.

Mohn und Gedächtnis

Here

Here—that means here, where the cherry blossom wants to be
  blacker than there.
Here—that means this hand, which helps it to be so.
Here—that means this ship, on which I came up the sand
  stream:
moored,
it lies in the sleep that you strewed.

Here—that means a man that I know:
his brow is white
like the embers he extinguished:
He threw his glass at my forehead
and came
when a year was up,
to kiss the scar.
He spoke of the curse and the blessing
and has said nothing since.

Here—that means this city
that is ruled from its evenings
by you and the cloud.

Von Schwelle zu Schwelle

Summer Report

The thyme carpet, by-passed
and no longer betrodden.
An empty line laid diagonally
across the bell-heath.
Nothing brought into the windfall.

Encounters again with
single words:
stone-break, hard-grass, time.

Sprachgitter

Flower

The stone.
The stone in the air, which I followed.
Your eye, as blind as the stone.

We were
hands,
we drained the darkness dry, found
the word that ascended the summer:
flower.

Growth.
Flower—a blindman's word.
Your eye and my eye:
they supply
the water.

Heart-wall by heart-wall
forms flowers.

One more word like that, and the hammers
will swing in the open.

Sprachgitter

All Souls' Day

What have I
done?
Inseminated the night, as if
there could be others, darker than
this.

Bird flight, stone flight, a thousand
described rotations. Gazes,
raped and culled. The sea,
tasted, drunk up, dreamt away. An hour,
soul-darkened. The next, an autumn light,
offered to a blind
feeling that passed that way. Others, many,
placeless and heavy themselves: seen and avoided.
Foundlings, stars,
black, full of language: named
after an oath that was silenced.

And once (when? that too is forgotten):
felt the barb
where the pulse ventured the counter-beat.

Sprachgitter

Psalm

No one molds us again out of earth and clay,
no one speaks into our dust.
No one.

Praise be to you, No one.
For your sake we
will bloom.
Toward
you.

A Nothing
we were, we are, we shall
remain, blooming:
the Nothing rose, the
No one's rose.

With
our stylus soul-clear,

our filament heaven-wasted,
our crown red
from the crimson word that we sang
over, oh over
the thorn.

Die Niemandsrose

Into the Rivers

Into the rivers north of the future
I cast out the net that you
hesitatingly load down
with shadows written
by stones.

Atemwende

Thread suns
above the gray-black wasteland.
A tree-
high thought
strikes the light-sound: there are
still songs to be sung beyond
humanity.

Atemwende

Standing, in the shadow
of the scar in the air.

Standing-for-no-one-and-nothing.
Unrecognized,
for you
alone.

With everything that has a place there,
even without
language.

Atemwende

No more sand art, no sand book, no masters.

The dice yielded nothing. How many
mute ones?
Seven-ten.

Your question—your answer.
Your song, what does it know?

Deepinsnow,
       Eepinno,
             E-i-o.

Atemwende

The broken-down taboos,
and the borderzone-being between them,
world-wet, in
search of meaning, in
flight from
meaning.

Fadensonnen

Soul-blind, behind the ashes,
in the sacred-senseless word,
the de-rhymed comes riding,
the brain-coat over its shoulders,

the auditory track vibrating
with moistened vowels,
it tears down the visual purple,
builds it up.

Fadensonnen

Wintered-on windfield: here
you must live, granular, pomegranate-like,
encrusted by
concealed prefrost,
the handwriting of the darkness in the midst

of the gold-yellow shadow—but never
were you only bird or fruit—
the star-spat
supersonic-wing
that you
sang out.

Fadensonnen

Vinegrowers dig up
the dark-houred clock,
depth by depth,

you glean and you read,

the Invisible
challenges the wind
to a joust,

you glean and you read,

the Openness bears
the stone behind its eye,
it will recognize you,
on the Sabbath.

Zeitgehöft

The Nothingness, for the
sake of our names
—they gather us in—,
sealed,

the end believes
the beginning,

the closed
clarity
testifies to
our silent
masters,
in the Indivisible.

Zeitgehöft

Pale-voiced, flayed
from the depths:
no word, no thing,
and of both the sole name,

ready for fall in you,
ready for flight in you,

wounded gain
of a world.

Lichtzwang

Webs between the words,

their timeyard—
a puddle,

gray-grated behind
the light-crest
meaning.

Lichtzwang

Notepad-pain,
snowed-on, over-snowed:

the newly-born
Nothingness
in the calendar-hole
lulls it, deludes it.

Lichtzwang

To speak with the blind alleys
from the other side,
from its
expatriated
meaning—:

to chew
this bread, with
writing teeth.

Schneepart

And power and pain
and what struck me
and drove and held:

Sound-leap-
years,

Fir-frenzy, at once,

the maddening conviction
that this could be said
differently.

Schneepart

Also raised
from the noises, ·
you demand—glass
becomes hostile, whatever
is more impenetrably yours—,
you demand everything
in its aura,

the dram of courage
becomes embittered,
watchful:
it knows that you know.

Schneepart

ALFRED GONG

Alfred Gong (1920–81), like Paul Celan and Rose Ausländer, was born in Chernovtsy, Bucovina, a one-time province of the Hapsburg Empire and today divided between Rumania and the Ukraine Republic of the Soviet Union. Like Celan and Ausländer, he emigrated after the war, first to Vienna in 1946 and then to the United States in 1951, where he lived in New York until his recent death. Although he was a loner and remained unrecognized on either side of the Atlantic, he corresponded from New York with Paul Celan in Paris. Gong's early poetry, which contains suggestions by Celan, is being edited for publication by Jerry Glenn at the University of Cincinnati. Gong is a strong poet, as exemplified by the selections here drawn from *Gnadenfrist* (Baden: Grasl, 1980).

Studium Generale

An *i* without dot:
the first letter we were taught to write,
while at the window the fly,
whose legs Peter had pulled off,
tried in vain to escape.

Before we could even read we were taught
that it's sweet to die for your country.
How sweet (sweet like honey, like halvah?
like the dark secret of your parents?)
no school-teacher taught us.

That the earth is round, we soon learned,
but that it's thorny like a hedgehog,
the stony egg, no one told us.
(It was then that Schnooky stole my stamp collection
and initiated me into Onan's mysteries)

We grew from Monday to Monday,
furnished the Roman statue with coal-black
eyes and Maria Stuart with a Napoleon-
beard (1933: my first long pair of pants and
the first pimples on my small forehead)

Later more useless stuff:
the Ten Commandments, for example, good for angels,
because conceived by them—impossible, however,
for human beings to follow in the straitjacket of
history. Further, six languages, three of them dead,
also the art of sophistry, dialectics, the Talmud—

There was, however, no adage that would later
appease the murderers. But when the leather-jacket
found the Phaidon in my basement,
despite my bloody lips I had to laugh.

Gnadenfrist

At that time

When Pan Silvester, our neighbor, died
and his dog also disappeared,
the gate to his garden responded
to my Open Sesame.

What remained of the summer's spectrum?
Immense green. The snake grass,
through which I looked anxiously,
for there stood the stone dwarf,
with beard and no nose, grinning.

The spheres ground stillness. Gold-blue
whizzed through the air. I buried
the dead butterfly in a coffin.
Soothingly came from somewhere
a breath of fountain and nut.
The noonday slept in the spider's web
on the red-currant branch.

In the shadow, sleep: good
like in mother's honeycomb. Shock
upon waking: a green dragon—
the caterpillar crawled on my knee.
My heart was calmed by the voice
of my sister looking for me.
Spellbound I watched the blackbird
as he drank from the basin.

Gnadenfrist

Somnia

In the shafts of sleep
the dams are covered with roughcast,
with signs that one recognizes and understands
before they drown in the light, with shadow,
shaken by images from other strange realms:

What defines the giantess
with the coral eye that emits rings
for which he must pay and pays until
his heart can no more? Where
does the ladder of roots lead? Why
did he run, the black egg in his hand,
chased by pool-greens? What was the name
of the city with the changing flag
over which he flew—then crashed, his
scream chained, into waking.

Later, as they came more seldomly, he realized:
with the genes one inherits also the dreams,
and sleep is a band, lit
now and then, between ice age and
end fire.

Gnadenfrist

Boedromion

Once more
to be able to say: September
and mean all Septembers
once and forever.

The pitcher on the threshhold.
Between door-hinge and jamb
breathes a spider web. Lose the way
home and tap out the sign of
September.

Already mobiles hover
above the smoldering thorn.
Soon your glove will count
the forsaken nests.

Then go. Without farewell, go
farther, go ahead and back:
He who doesn't flee from
September in September remains
there imprisoned a hundred winters.

Extricate yourself. Give it up
and blot out the sleep-word
September.

Gnadenfrist

[Translator's note: The title is the name of a month in the Ionian calendar, which is associated with the festival of the god Apollo Boedromios.]

Echo

From the dunes of your hair—your voice
whispering above the horizon, around the gnomes
of your hair—your voice frozen
in amber—your hair, it breathes, it crawls
over whetstone and graves, it rustles
a mild word, ensnares my finger,
entangles itself in rods and nets, sweeps
autumn from the aisle, dissolves itself
in Boreas, in the mirror, foggy with

syllables—your language from a strange face—
the strands in a floating bottle—

Where did your hair take you? Where
did the lure take me?

Your hair for sale in the showcase
—between star-fish and sparrow-hawk—
without blood without shame without cry.

Gnadenfrist

Failure

Enough blarney about love and death!
We have well survived
elegiac vespers
limited temptation
love feast à la carte
exercises from Kama Sutra
for advanced beginners
under rotating mirrors.

We exchanged vows, recorded on tape,
endowed ourselves with new names
—I Phoenix   you Matrix—
and gave to revolt the parole:
Love, endlessly love, without mercy!

Sleep, go to sleep at last.
You have given up yourselves.
No call can bring us from the swelling—
step down, no promise.
Only the smell of a worm-eaten apple
enlivens
the provisional end of the world.

Gnadenfrist

Thanaton Melein

You with yourself.
Nothing—only
the shadow of snowfall.

The night unravels
your time.
You leave behind no vacancy.

In front of the gate the day
advances,
its finger on retreat.

Quartered in the window
the calm
of a surrendered city.

Gnadenfrist

[Translator's note: Although the form of the Greek in the title remains unclear, Gong apparently intended the meaning "Preparation for Death," as indicated by a notebook entry. I am indebted to Jerry Glenn for this information.]

Limbo

No longer can the ear
differentiate
the sea from its own heartbeat.
The rain behind the glass:
a movie from the twenties
uninterrupted.

He who passes up life
sells himself
and is damned to trek back and forth
in the occluded tunnel
dream-blind and strange.

No There and no Then.
This eternity again and again.

Gnadenfrist

Ultra

Under you shrivels
a blue ball that bore
the heavy name *earth*.

Soon you recognize
it, nailed to the cross
of the south, the out-witted

God. In his dimming one-eye
are gathered the fires of his
eclipsed earth.

Gnadenfrist

Robinson

listens
to the falling snow
on the island of Manhattan.

Too listless to open letters,
too tired to write.
Only occasionally
a dream recalls
the earlier strangeness.

Across the street
black Ms. Friday
is telephoning.

Gnadenfrist

DORIS MÜHRINGER

Doris Mühringer (1920–   ) began in the tradition and developed a highly individual voice, expressing existential concerns in hermetic form. She lives today as a free-lance writer and translator in Vienna. Selections are from *Gedichte II* (Wien: Österreichische Verlagsanstalt, 1969), *Staub öffnet das Auge* (Graz: Styria, 1976), and the journal *Literatur und Kritik* (1981).

On the Death of Paul Celan (A Vindication)

I

Again one
Again one of the seismographs
of the world
overladen
We should acquire
more callous
antennae
We should become
more robust
instruments
But
should we?

II

Root-tips in the centre
where the world shakes
butterfly-flower
burns
peacock's cry
till the end

Papillon
singed by fire
assuaged by water

Human sacrifice

With open eye
stretched out
painless at last

Staub öffnet das Auge

Do Not Lock Your House

Do not lock your house
when you go to speak with the dead.
One—who knows?—is already on the way,
one who will enter—

He will tend your fire,
your heart,
the lamp, burned low, in the gateway:
so that you return!

He will listen a long time
to the voices in the woodwork,
to the flight of birds,
before he follows you.

Gedichte II

Waiting

Waiting
Wind
changes
Storm
opens the eye
The
curtain
trembles
Waiting

Ashes might fall
on the gown
Ashes might fall
on the death-gown

Waiting

Dust
opens the eye

Staub öffnet das Auge

To Stay*

To stay
means
to take a different direction
To take a different direction
means
to get by with
the same water under your feet
the same wind in your nostrils
the same weapons between your teeth

Still
stay
turn
perhaps find a way out
run ashore perhaps
on the silkbeach
once
on the other bank

*In navigation to change the course of a sailing vessel.

or

there still remains
flight:
hard turn
let's stay
into the wind
turn
into the storm
set all sails
hey
spit out the weapons
laughter between the teeth
adorns us:
whitely whitely shines the reef ahead
glorious scimitar
stern-faced mistress
who will encircle us
who will embrace us
who will possess us
finally

Infinitely

Staub öffnet das Auge

Les enfants du paradis

But then came the angels
the lovely the luring
the birds
and let me in
to them
and they sang:
Fly with us
sister ours
fly
and we flew
and thus they sang on:
In the sleep-skies above
sounding sleep-skies above
our king he sees you
he sees you
fly
and we flew

and in the sleep-skies above
sounding sleep-skies above
they stopped singing my siblings
and fell upon me
and devoured
les enfants du paradis
my name
and the roots of my eyes
and the root of my tongue
then I stopped screaming

And thus
they brought their nests
into the cavities of my head

Staub öffnet das Auge

Lost Goldfish in Dream

Lost goldfish in dream
from my eyes
asked Robinson
but he had not seen them
dug in the South Sea
but there were only pearls
asked the wind but he
was in love with the palms
and pushed me away
Went to my mother under the earth
and there they sat
in her eyes
one in the left, one in the right
and the other in the middle
of her brow and wagged their tales

Staub öffnet das Auge

Dalmatian Ballad

Let's celebrate the feast of the red horse
and board the boat, young brother,

leave the white sail, let be the lute—
the wing-beat of large birds will carry us
and nets, in which we once caught fish,
will sing, and sickle scales, young brother,
will dance before us on the water.

Let go the garland—Don't you know that seaweed
adorned us long ago! Deep in our eyes
dwell pearls, and from our heart, young brother,
whereof the yellow moon long ate its fill,
rise joyously the coral reefs,
a thousand joyous coral reefs, young brother,
and they will pierce the fat and yellow moon.

Gedichte II

I Have a House

Have a house
have a roof on the house
have a window in the roof on the house
have snow on the house
have snow on the roof on the house
have snow on the window in the roof on the house
have it light under the snow on the window in the roof on the
    house
have it warm under the snow on the roof on the house
have it quiet under the snow on the house
have it quiet under the snow

Staub öffnet das Auge

To Sing in the Darkness

In the rain
I came
I.
In the rain
I went
an other.

Was
who went in the green
I.
Am
who goes out of the green
an other.

Caught a doe in the green
enclosed and embraced her:
I.
Slaughtered her
cut up and ate her:
an other.

Out of the rain
I came
I.
Into the rain
I went
an other.

Literatur und Kritik

owl
you
my frightful friend
of the darkness
nothing reveals
STILLISTHELAKETHELITTLEBIRDSSLEEP
nothing reveals
till a sound of death
your presence
foe

Gedichte II

FRANZ RICHTER

Franz Richter (1920–   ) is a native of Vienna, where he currently resides as teacher and writer. Like many of the Austrian literati, he writes also for literary programs on the radio, since the radio assumes the central role in life there that television does in American life. Current selections are from *Trockengebiet* (Baden: Grasl, 1980).

Memorial in Aachen

1914–1918
1939–1945

a flame dances in the stone lamp
to those unnamed intervals
only the pantomime of the fire,
flaming up in a raid of force
against the darkness,
exhausted in smoke,
inferno of light.

Trockengebiet

Night Flight

At night I have wings.
They grow quickly in the dark
after I wave goodbye
to the here and now.

But the day with its scissors
of light clips them back.
Then I hop around and peck corn
in the sand, small ballast
in hope of flight.

Trockengebiet

Course of Life

Corduroy road, unfit for biking
or free-footed walking,
headstrong, unsteady
is the course of my life.

Yet:
only my uneven will
makes it such.
If my non-will were perfect,
empty, pure, and round,
a center for the world's axis,
then I too would roll
easily, unruefully
toward the goal.

Trockengebiet

ILSE AICHINGER

Ilse Aichinger (1921–   ) is known primarily as an author of prose and radio plays. As one of the first writers after the Second World War, she won wide acclaim with her novel *Die grössere Hoffnung* (Frankfurt: Fischer, 1948), as well as for her short stories, such as "Spiegelgeschichte" (1954). Her excellence with short forms is evident also in poetry, and the volume *verschenkter Rat* (Frankfurt: Fischer, 1978) presents a collection of poems written between 1958 and 1978.

March

The gray cows
trot down over the roofs,
the shadows of trees,
the tattered sun tracks
keep in step with the graves.
The women at the windows
concede,
soon it will rain,
our consent
is always presupposed.

verschenkter Rat

135

A Walk

Since the world arose out of distances,
stairways, and marshlands,
and the bearable becomes suspicious,
don't let
the magpies fly up suddenly
behind your stalls and plunge
shiningly into the shiny pond,
don't let
your smoke rise
in front of the woods,
let's wait, rather, until the golden fox
appear in the snow.

verschenkter Rat

Abroad

Books from strange libraries,
the strengthened doves.
If it depends on
the places we
are able to leave,
with their raspberry bushes,
their linens
that fold in the wind;
they change quietly behind us,
while we stay,
on the warm backs
of gardens, stony
or of sand.

verschenkter Rat

Last Night

For what should appear
but patches of snow,
swords on the edge of childhood
and toward the forest

the branches of apple trees
that the moon washed black,
the hens that are counted?

verschenkter Rat

Game of Cards

Forgetting the dark corners
faces
and the gold under the wall,
we leave everything there,
the swing with the ice men,
the patterns that blinded us,
and under the kitchen bench
the rhinoceros, warmed by the light.

verschenkter Rat

Thirteen Years

The cottage party is long past,
the sheen of chestnut trees,
lined up at the window of the garden house.
And still in the room
the candle,
the religions of the world.

The desert dust under the bicycle hose.
After this noon
the twilight comes more quickly.
The companions
and a green grave,
Rajissa.

We'll come again in the evening,
we'll never come again.

verschenkter Rat

Counted out

The day you
came into the ice without shoes,
the day
the two calves
were driven to slaughter,
the day I
shot through my left eye,
but no longer,
the day
the butchers' newspaper reported
that life continues
the day it did.

verschenkter Rat

Attempt

Between ladder and north wall,
visit in the afternoon and discarded wood,
left-over apple and snow
to establish a relation
that is indissoluble.

verschenkter Rat

Wish

To learn silence
from the shortened visits,
from the dark woods,
the unused middle rooms,
from the girls in their white dresses,
columns of dust that support temples,
from doors in shimmering mirrors.

verschenkter Rat

Village Path

The starlings slander in the fall
and sometimes I hear the doors close twice,
once in dream.

Who gave us the images
the red apples
in the garden of the charcoal burner,
unrhymed, but sunned to lie with us.

verschenkter Rat

Part of the Question

The water stands high on the place,
the air still rises in bubbles,
but what they sing
doesn't reach me any more.
The fish circle round the church doors,
who gives me an answer:
Should I go to the mountain
or into the house to those
who love me,
and the far-away look,
the grating of footsteps
once again?
How black my land becomes,
but deep below, time
writhes greenly.

verschenkter Rat

Self-Made

I'll let my villages stand
without words
and open at the fences
and let the snow
whirl through.
From the height of my granaries

I want to watch the jaguars,
hear the wolves whistle.
The sun sprang away here,
but the children
are helped in their harvest
by dandelions,
Place for a King!

verschenkter Rat

H. C. ARTMANN

h.c. artmann (1921–   ) is a many-sided writer, as well as something of a legend. As initiator of the Vienna Group in 1953, he was one of the first Austrians to write "experimental poetry," and he wrote the revolutionary document of the Vienna Group, "Eight-Point Proclamation of the Poetic Act," in collaboration with Konrad Bayer. Artmann is known also for his innovative dialect poems, ballads, and dramatic forms. His poetry, which often arose spontaneously on his minstrel-like travels through Europe, was collected by G. Binsinger in *ein lilienweisser brief aus lincolnshire* (Frankfurt: Suhrkamp, 1969).

Eight-Point Proclamation of the Poetic Act (1953)

It is an unassailable proposition that one can be a poet without ever having written a word.

This however presupposes the desire, felt more or less strongly, to want to act poetically. The alogical gesture itself, carried out in this way, can be raised to an act of perfect beauty, yes, to poetry. Beauty, however, is a concept that will be used here in a greatly expanded sense.

1. The poetic act is poetry that rejects all second-hand inventions, that is, reproductions of any sort, be it of language, music, or writing.

2. The poetic act is poetry solely for the sake of poetry. It is pure poetry and free from all external ambitions for recognition, praise, or criticism.

3. A poetic act is made public sometimes only by chance; that, however, happens only once in a hundred times. In any case, because of its beauty and purity, the poetic act should not occur with the intention of becoming public, for it is an act of the heart and of pagan indifference.

4. The poetic act is consciously improvised and is anything but merely a poetic situation—which would render poetry superfluous. Any idiot can find himself in such a situation, without however necessarily becoming aware of it.

5. The poetic act is a pose in its noblest form, free from conceit and full of humorous humility.

6. To the honorable masters of the poetic act we reckon first of all the satanic-elegiac C. D. Nero and above all our man, the humanly-philosophical Don Quixote.

7. The poetic act is materially completely worthless and thus from the start never conceals the bacillus of prostitution. Its disinterested consummation is simply noble.

8. The consummated poetic act, inscribed in our memory, is one of the few riches we carry with us that cannot be taken away.

Wiener Gruppe

interior. . .

at first it is a constellation
inside a gruesome shepherd-legend
the juniper tree still blooms
and the girls go down to the river to bathe.
then it's the moon woven into a carpet
or into the wind
or the shy whisper of the mandrake
a puzzling spice-seed on the wings of the evening.
in view of the sister-gallows you are wildly awakened
by the gold-leafed plummet of flying doves.
then comes a gentler image
and an evening chime over the sea-dark lagoon
a magic bone finally
that I forgot to adorn. . .

ein lilienweisser brief

every evening a counterfeit minstrel
draws the rich curving material of your thoughts
through the deserts of numismatic salons.
picture frames wrapped with strips of paper
absorb the deeper level of being
from a formerly unvolatile past nature.
afterwards on the other side a bird statue peers
(integrated into the middle of the underestimations)
as in the security places of architecture
when the maximum crash-speed
is extremely exceeded.

ein lilienweisser brief

salt and bread in our
hands pray
when it rains lions
and hermits
chop
nocturnal wood
when coastlines
move
and forgotten hills
press into the
deep nakedness of spring
when the bird-encircled
shaft of the ginkgo
sprouts the beautiful
ideogram of miracles. . .
how exemplary is
our apparent lostness
in the saving plural
of changed winds.

ein lilienweisser brief

oh, anselm,
take
schubert
out of the disco,
the evening

approaches
on flannel
soles
shh!
the thrush
has finished
its song
and the tea
dreams complete
in the kitchen. . .
anselm
jumps up
breaking
his shoelaces
then when he
and his antonia
take tea
and are proper
a wonderful needle
scratches
sonata numero twelve
in the contemplative
beginning
of a yet-to-come
evening

ein lilienweisser brief

now look here . . !
a little dove comes
to the windowsill
and holds
a postcard
in his beak . . .
you must pay
postage due
antonia
your friend
is poor . . .
he has
put
only half
the postal fee
on his card . . .

but you
antonia
because you
are so beautiful
i exempt you
from half
the postage due . . .
that is exactly
one quarter of the amount
which your lover
should have paid . . .
dear antonia!
your anselm
who loves you
so dearly
sends you many
many kisses
thinks of you
and would like to be
with you . . .
ah
how happy i am
says antonia
that it is spring . . !
and reimbursed
the little dove
flies away
from the windowsill . . .
whir!!!
over roofs and
towers!
over casemates
and brothels!
over graveyards
and merry-go-rounds!
over giants and
dwarfs and mongrels!
over cabbage heads
and cannibals!
over living and
dead and ghosts
over islands and
ships and dockyards
over negroes and indians
and silver lions
all the way
to anselm—

and says:
next time
it won't go
so smoothly without the
right postage . . !

ein lilienweisser brief

when my anselm
drifts away
from me,
says antonia,
then there always
arises
an assyrian angel
from the pillars
of nineveh. . .
the olive leaf
is withered
and dried,
no bird
calls
from the reeds and
in the northwest
there forms
a tiny little
cloud:
a wrinkle
in the corner
of my left eye,
a small bastard
of sorrow and
loving anger. . .

ein lilienweisser brief

mon dieu mon dieu
what has
happened?
in his old
napoleon hat

anselm carries
a wounded
nightingale. . .
but the questions
that then rain down!
how did it come to this?
how could that happen. . .
you poor little bird
imagine
if anselm
had not
found you
but everything
is okay again. . . and:
tra la la!
the shepherds' flutes
on the prairie
will soon sleep. . .
not even imaginable
if anselm
were not here
says antonia—
adieu philosophy
and up and away
to the happy
1×1 of the night. . .
today we want
to take
all cages
from the trees. . !
stop stop stop
what is this. . .
where do you get out
you tight-rope walkers
and acrobats. . .
your exercises
make me
nauseated!
quit it. . .
breaking a leg
is a fate
three times as
tough
in the spring;
or be it
for the sake of
heavenly peace

that I'm asking you:
even the moon
goes through the gardens
why then
do you want
to go on ropes
through the air?
I'll give you
a silver piece
immediately
if you'll stop
that recklessness. . .

ein lilienweisser brief

my heart

my heart is the smiling dress of a never-guessed idea
my heart is the mute question of an ivory arch
my heart is the fresh snow on the tracks of young birds
my heart is the gesture, evening-quiet, of a breathing hand
my heart lies in sparkling white boxes of muslin
my heart drinks shining yellow water from the emerald cup
my heart bears a strange animal circle of the tenderest gold
my heart beats joyfully in the loose rain of the mid-winter star

ein lilienweisser brief

o death you dark master
you elixir bitter as gall
you itinerant harpoonist and god
you moon full of blind eyes
you rose-dwarf in ambush
you spider-tower you spider
you point to dethroned life
o death you dark master
hear us hear us
spare us
from your brittle coffins
don't bite our brains like glass
o death you dark master

don't bite us like glass. . .
o death you dark master
you gaping jaw bone
you disconsolate-laden earth
you unformed rat snout
you thoroughly wormed flesh
you seed glutton you empty shell
you wet ash-sun
o death you dark master
hear us hear us
spare us
from your galled coffins
don't bite our brains like glass
o death you dark master
don't bite us like glass. . .

ein lilienweisser brief

ERICH FRIED

Erich Fried (1921–   ), writing from his postwar residence in London, is one of the most publicized and most popular of German-speaking poets. Sociopolitical agitation and self-investigation are the major themes of his highly readable poetry. Among the numerous volumes, which appear almost annually, selections are from *Anfechtungen* (1967) and *Die Freiheit den Mund aufzumachen* (1972), both at Berlin: Wagenbach.

Upon Re-reading a Poem by Paul Celan

"there are
still songs to be sung beyond
humanity"*

Reading
after your death
the pregnant lines
tied together
in your clear knots
drinking the bitter images
coming upon—
painful as previously—
the awful error
in your poem that they praised
the uninviting

---

*[Translator's note: from Celan's poem "Fadensonnen" in *Atemwende*.]

150

invitation
to Nothingness

Songs
certainly
also beyond
our death
Songs of the future
beyond the terrible times
in which we are entangled
A singing beyond
the humanly conceivable
Vast

But not a single song
beyond humanity

Die Freiheit den Mund aufzumachen

Deserted Room

The dust in the room
gentle on the windowpanes
the quiet dust
on the table
on the old pillow:
peach fluff
that strokes
the stroking hand
that shows the sun
the way through closed windows

To be tired
and not want to cry
and not want
to die
to have cried and already be dead:
In the light dust
that shows the sunshine the way
to lie on the pillow
not again
no—always
still always
and already for ever
dust on dust under dust

Dust on the table
on the bed
on the windowpanes:
dust in the dust
sun in the dust
dust in the sun
I—dust in the room of the sun
I—dust on the pillow
I Again I Still I Always
in the room of dust

Anfechtungen

Rural

It's beautiful here
The girls are like young
trees and many trees
are like dancing girls

Here I want to
take heart and try
to compose myself
and look for myself

and almost without fear
for I know that
I am
not here

Anfechtungen

Description of a Landscape

Colors of childhood
birds against the sun
shiny grass in front of the woods
my only seeing and hearing

The more often I describe you
and the more I seek you
the farther and paler
and more amorphous you become

I hear the rustling
of my words from the rustling of the woods
I see the gray and the green
of faces and clothes

They praise my good memory
and sound me out
they eat the light and shadow
they drink the wind

Anfechtungen

Speechless

Why do you
still write
poems
although you
reach only
a few people
by this method

friends ask me
impatient because
they reach only
a few people
by their methods

and I don't
have an answer
for them

Die Freiheit den Mund aufzumachen

Revenue

To gather hope
from solvable problems
from possibilities
from everything
that promises something

To save
strength
for that
which needs
to be done

Thus the supply
of unused
despair grows
quietly

Anfechtungen

Goal Consciousness

For tactical reasons
I must have humor
since I can't win friends
for the cause
that concerns us
through grim seriousness
or inability to laugh

For tactical reasons
I must be generous
since I can't win friends
for the cause
that concerns us
through brute hostility
or callous indifference

If these considerations
are the motivation
for my cultivation
of these useful characteristics
then my generosity
looks just like
my humor

Die Freiheit den Mund aufzumachen

ALOIS VOGEL

Alois Vogel (1922–   ) has many voices, from existential-philosophical to social-critical. He is also active in literary circles and serves as editor of a journal and a book series. His development was unusual in that it went from prose to poetry. He has in the past two decades published several volumes of poetry, including *Sprechen und Hören* (1971) and *Im Auge das Wissen* (1976), both at München: Delp. Selections here are from his recent work as it appeared in *Literatur und Kritik* (1983) and *Podium* (1974).

With Closed Eyes

1

Lying
Lying as if dead
Lying on one's back
With closed eyes
looking
at the questioning beams
of the goats
comrades of childhood
Grinding teeth
above the symmetry
Staring pupils
above the painful grade sheet
of the school report
above the quietly disappearing footsteps

of the faltering track
through the snow
Black beams
above the poplar avenue of friends
in a vineyard
stormed by barbarians

2

Lying
Lying as if dead
Lying on one's back
With closed eyes
hearing
only the quavering cries
of the screech owl
from the walnut tree on the other side
Beethoven's Seventh
and Gustav Mahler's
slow movement
from "Lied von der Erde"
in between Franz Liszt
"Les Préludes"
The howling
above the bay in the wilderness
the death rattle of horse bones
surrounded by the humming hunger
of freed flies
and enslaved peoples

3

Lying
Lying as if dead
Lying on one's back
With closed eyes
feeling
the throbbing of the pulse
in one's temples
the sweet taste
of ripe nuts
the dryness of wine
olives and fish
and the freshness of flesh
in a bite of watermelon

the wrinkles
of figs
melting on one's tongue
Finally lying again
Lying with closed eyes
Feeling only the throbbing
of the pulse

4

Lying
Lying on one's back
with closed eyes
with deaf ears
silenced pulse
ground down in the symmetry
of the constantly moving jaws
Gone into
the black beams
of the pupils
Before long
snow will fall

Literatur und Kritik

Situation

Increasingly
it crumbles away
Soon it will reach you
Soon you will be washed away
Sunk
somewhere
that you don't know

Appeared
placed there
a lighthouse, you thought
a polestar
a chandelier
in the middle of the land
on a mountain

The hounds
raised their leg
The crows
defecated
The mole
went his way
The rain
dug a thousand ditches

Increasingly roots
grasp into the emptiness
Streams carry the earth away
Rivers move the rubble around
The breakers beat on the shore
Still a thin blade of grass holds

Podium

HERBERT ZAND

Herbert Zand (1923–70) is remembered as a keen observer of culture and a defender of humanistic values, which he expressed also in novelistic and essay form. His works were posthumously collected and published by Wolfgang Kraus, including a volume of poetry written between 1949 and 1970 entitled *Aus zerschossenem Sonnengeflecht* (Wien: Europa, 1973).

Continually

He who has no house and no home to return to,
only suns here and there
and perhaps
an angel
where otherwise no angel
watches over the corn,
he must continually depend on the infinite.
But the angels of death
touch his head and his hands
continually with black wings,
close his eyes continually
when he opens them, tear all earthly things
from his fists with their storm-yellow beaks,
chop up the scream when he screams
so that a terrible shriek results,
and the fear he endures
makes his face ugly.
Alone he dies into the nameless.
Only a word from him remains

that descendants believe in:
hope continually, continually
hope and sometime deliverance.

Aus zerschossenem Sonnengeflecht

Pain

Pure white, placeless.
Filtered out of the sun,
who knows when,
then fermentation, turbidity.

There are descriptions, things said
about recognition:
but not yet
I still don't
I still don't recognize

The prophets saw
traces
in the entrails,
pure writing, speechless.
I don't read them.
I experience them
like hemlock
like poison, like the sharpness
of time.

I don't
I still don't
I don't recognize again
I don't interpret
what was in front of me,
what announces itself, penetrates
into emptiness, out of which, haltingly,
my breath falls back.

Aus zerschossenem Sonnengeflecht

The Gardener

My flower beds were trampled down
            during the night by nymphs and fauns,
and they braided my most beautiful flowers
            into their hair.
That is the case today and tomorrow—
            what I prepare during the day
this wanton rabble destroys at night.

I can't change any of that:
            my garden lies in their path,
and they don't deviate from it.
            First I wanted to fight, then to flee
finally I acquiesced in defiance—

            Now they gratefully
do me this service, and I often wake up in the morning,
            find a small plant—
inconspicuous and fragile—
            yet it blooms already in the evening.
When did this world ever see
            such calyx and color?

Aus zerschossenem Sonnengeflecht

My Poor Exploited Language

My poor exploited language,
how often you have been the thin thread
on which I saved myself,
the straw,
the coat in winter,
water in the desert
and daily bread.

You, the beginning of knowledge,
first warmth of joy,
articulation of my anxiety
and sometime companion on byroads—

let's graze peacefully like two old war horses
side by side, this and that still remains to be said.

Aus zerschossenem Sonnengeflecht

Waiting. . .

Waiting. . . .
while the earth
            dances around itself
with a thousand butterflies
that tumble through light and warmth,
waiting here
with an impatient heart
that conceives worlds
a thousand times greater than
            the heavens of priests.
Waiting
here and today
with butterfly heart
with restlessness
            with sadness
with the image of gods
in a quake of fear
in a drum-fire of joy
that suddenly breaks loose
            and extinguishes everything
that was a lie,
waiting for breakthrough
waiting. . .

Waiting. . . .
while the earth turns
the evening light of the world
surrounded by thousands of butterflies,
waiting here
with an impatient heart
that conceives worlds
a thousand times greater than
            the heavens of priests
waiting, here and today
with butterfly heart
            with the restlessness
            with the sadness
            with the image of gods
caught in a horizon of eyes
in a quake of fear
in a drum-fire of joy
that suddenly breaks loose
            and extinguishes everything
that was a lie,
            waiting. . .

Aus zerschossenem Sonnengeflecht

I have a Wild Desire to Die

I have a wild desire to die
and go into the clouds, where
the lightning is and the warm thunderstorms.
I believe you will be there in every drop,
in the warmth, in the wind that blows the clouds,
and I will be in the light that shines through the clouds,
and in the air that warms you.
And when you fall I will be
the earth that catches you. And you
will be grass through which I rise,
and I will be in the blood of the animals
through which you flow, and the eye
through which you enter, thousandfold refracted, as light
and as image, and as image I will enter the image you are.

I have a wild desire to live
after a thousand deaths that again and again
transform me into that which you love,
which awakens your love, which transforms you,
which enters and dies in me and becomes the innermost
chamber of my heart.

Sleep, love, rocked by the soft
pulse of our terrible life,
above the dream's theaters that all perform you
and tear you into a hundred plays and remake you again;
may the endless, the infinite preserve you.
I'll send you my death angel, my life angel,
he still has time to be gentle to you like a child
so that he may enter your ruins
and strangely and wonderfully
take your light into his
and light up whatever you wish.

I'll send you my death angel, my life angel,
he has time and goes idly so that he may be the one
who is gentle to you like a child,
who chokes you, who chases and throws you down,
binds you with chains in the fire and hunts you with dogs,
and I will be restless while dreaming and scream.
Sleep, love, into the harshness of the gray morning
in which your hate awakens anew and throws
itself against the world in order to injure it,
and the dirty water runs on your temples, disgusting,
and the cooing pigeons mock your love.
Oh, that you wanted to be good! That you carried

your love through the street gutters that betray everything.
Morning. Blindly I search for your hand.

Aus zerschossenem Sonnengeflecht

GERHARD FRITSCH

Gerhard Fritsch (1924–69) is a prominent poet, and he was also a literary figure, editor of leading journals in the 1960s. A participant in a transition period—and also affected by it—his active life ended in suicide. His strong lyric talent found expression in four volumes of poetry, published between 1952 and 1962 and collected in *Gesammelte Gedichte* (Salzburg: O. Müller, 1978).

Fear

From the beginning you were there,
Fear, in the face of man.
The gatherer, the hunter, the herder,
the ploughman, and warrior, all knew you,
most constant companion to progress of questionable ages.
You created for us the deities, cities, and laws,
you were the will-o'-the-wisp of Germany's swamps,
the night that cried out from the Congolese jungles,
the siren that sang on the wood of Athenian galleys,
changeable animal, you went pregnant
around fox-hole, fortress, and castle.
We named you with a thousand names
and wanted to banish you forever, house god of every faith,
to the secure fireside corner
of the finitely fathomed outline of our heart:
there you stood up colossal,
single eagle of the century,

and with the first flap of your wings
silently knocked the groundplan
out of our prayerless fingers.

Gesammelte Gedichte

I thought myself to be guest

I thought myself to be guest in many faces
and then saw that it was always only a shadow
that fell for a while on the curtain of a stranger.
Not the friend with whom I tore up the pictures of childhood,
not the others who later filled my days,
not the comrade with whom I escaped from the war,
not the others whom I had met earlier
near the ground as brothers of fate,
nor the women I loved and to whom I was lover,
since then, as a last summer's full moon
hung burning above the forest—nothing, nothing—
nothing brought deliverance from my self.

I remained locked in my loneliness,
and every release, as good as it seemed, was deceit.
I learned from quiet books of sad wisdom
that in truth a person always remains alone
because he can never break down the walls of his soul.
Only the longing seems to conquer them,
but the longing is only a dream . . .

Now I am suddenly guest in your face
and feel, like a wonder far from rash intoxication of sense,
feel how all the gates of my soul open slowly
and something silent goes over to you
into your biding smile—
is it now real,
truly real?

Gesammelte Gedichte

Upon Listening to the Third Brandenburg Concerto

The colors fade,
the world becomes night.
Only the stubble fields still shine
for a while toward the south.
The colors fade, the paths disappear,
the colors were weak, the paths were false,
only food for death grew in the fields;
the colors have deceived us,
the paths have led us astray,
they led us into the wilderness
and we went weakly
we went blindly
into the depths of the night.

I lean on the window.
The colors have faded,
the paths have disappeared—
that there are stars above?
Do we then still
deserve this favor:
Music?

Gesammelte Gedichte

Poppy

Fluttering red,
brightest in the meadow,
boldest, most changeable flower,
you in the silver manes of the meadow
single impatience!
Poppy,
more luminous than light,
more flaming than flames,
the earth
burns itself
gives itself
in you
to the sky full of wind.
Remaining is only

the black capsule
of bitter poison.

Gesammelte Gedichte

Look in the Landscape

Red and soft the grass rustles
under the wind, and I look out over the meadow
and the paths that lose themselves in the folds
of the woods like the sparkling
of stones in the evening that
gradually lifts itself up from the valleys,
invisible vapor carried by wind.

The mountains emerge more clearly
in the distance, red and soft
like the grass from its litanies—
and out there, at once so far and so near
I see you on the crest of the meadow
and I know without wonder: this is
the hour of miracles.

And I begin to go
through the rustling grass,
through the evening vapors,
through the past time of the valleys,
up into the light of the distance,
into the great landscape of breakthrough
in which the light does not go out
as long as you are there.

I go
through the rustling grass,
through the past time of the valleys,
carried by wind
into your light.

Stay . . .

Gesammelte Gedichte

Words persistently

Words persistently
demanding, naming,
given much too quickly
to opinions, formulas, and judgments,
words, failing again and again
already in front of the shadow that the pen
casts on this paper—
words,
echoless from the things,
bridge to being continually collapsing,
ruins, skillfully sawed into conventions,
remains, quickly walled up into small chapels
of phrases (wanderer, off-with-the-hat, a poem),
but the dove in them is always only of plaster;
words: wanting completely only the origin.
That, however, indestructible like the flight of letters
often in curves, crosses, and circles on the edge,
in the childlike pure arabesque of our failure
in face of the first upbeat of the alpha
of reality.

Gesammelte Gedichte

Why the many words?

They don't nail down
what does not let me rest,
they can't contain
what drives me to speak.
What then are dream figures
forced into words?

Gesammelte Gedichte

Afternoon

Slowly
the curtain flutters
between garden and room.

A violet phlox-star falls
soundlessly
beside the vase.

Outside
behind the curtain
stands a giant
and breathes.

Softly and carefully
and deadly.

Gesammelte Gedichte

Judas

When it's Easter, someone
must play Judas. Whether
the lot falls to him or whether
he volunteers is not important
for the action. It doesn't matter
if he plays his role
badly: he ends up on the tree.
We breathe a sigh of relief, this time
we have concealed our ability
to play Judas,
whether it's Easter
or not.

Gesammelte Gedichte

Saint Maria Maggiore

Saint Maria Maggiore
on the postcards: stern cupola
in the evening sky of the laguna.
Curious, we come from all over,
women with bare arms, men with
chewing gum and boredom in their mouths.
We feed the doves
and find the droves of cats cute or demonic,
gloating between the decay of the stones,

we pay admission to dei Frari
and fees for the Bridge of Sighs,
we ride in a gondola and drink espresso and know
for a moment at least when
the sun sentimentally
drowns in the sea
that we have the plague and no faith,
that you will come to our aid
if our steamboat sirens
in the harbor
call for help.

Gesammelte Gedichte

Sunflowers in October

Along the fence
the heavy sun-heads
the bright ones
have turned black.

Merrily singing,
the birds have
carelessly
stolen the face of summer
when it wanted
carefully
to remove the cobweb veils.

Other birds,
black,
like the blind heads,
crouch on fences without meaning
in the harvest-destroyed world.

Even the yellow asters
do not bring back
fulfillment.

Gesammelte Gedichte

August Night

Once again the smell of hay
reaped by the low moon,
but also the mown grain
like haze from the river,
and the many stars
that fall from the sky.

No one
goes looking for them.
In the fog the thistles grow.

Gesammelte Gedichte

Between Evening and Night

The villages are going away now.
Further, the lanterns become
their night hat. The small chaste ones
go as the last.

Don't be afraid.
The forest, it remains there
with its fox and dove,
with deer and snake.
Between the trunks it weaves
for them a colorless cloth
of fog and sleep.

Death
went away with the villages
when you came
between evening and night.

Gesammelte Gedichte

FRIEDERIKE MAYRÖCKER

Friederike Mayröcker (1924–   ) is among the most prominent Austrian authors writing today, individually and in collaboration with Ernst Jandl. She was associated with the Vienna Group of "experimental poetry" in the 1960s and has continued to develop as a highly imaginative writer of both prose and poetry. Selections are from *Tod durch Musen* (Reinbek: Rowohlt, 1966) and *In langsamen Blitzen* (Berlin: Literarisches Colloquium, 1974), as reprinted in *Ausgewählte Gedichte* (Frankfurt: Suhrkamp, 1979). Also represented are poems from her recent volume, *Gute Nacht, guten Morgen* (Frankfurt: Suhrkamp, 1982).

Ostia will receive you

i will be in Ostia
i will expect you there
i will embrace you there
i will hold your hand in Ostia
i will be there
in Ostia
is the mouth of the Tiber
the old river

i will not be in Ostia
i will not expect you there
i will not embrace you there
i will not hold your hand in Ostia
i will not be there
in Ostia

is the mouth of the old river
the Tiber

Tod durch Musen

Will wither like grass
also my hand and the pupil of my eye
will wither like grass • my foot and my hair my softest word
will wither like grass • your mouth your mouth
will wither like grass • your seeing in me
will wither like grass • my cheek my cheek and the small
    flower
that you know there will wither like grass
will wither like grass • your mouth your crimson-colored
    mouth
will wither like grass • but the night but the fog but the
    fullness
will wither like grass will wither like grass

Tod durch Musen

what I call you
when I think about you
and you are not there:

my wild strawberry
my sugar-lizard
my comfort-bag
my silk-spinner
my care-chaser
my aurelia
my stone-flower
my slumber-child
my morning-hand
my full-forgetter
my window-bar
my moon-hider
my silver staff
my evening glow
my sun-thread

my snouted hare
my stag head
my rabbit foot
my stairway-frog
my chandelier
my spring thief
my shaky nag
my silver snail
my ink well
my broom-fox
my tree-cutter
my storm-deflector
my bear-keeper
my tooth-pointer
my horse ear
my park tree
my ring-horn
my monkey pocket
my winter turn
my artichoke
my midnight
my backwards-counter

(da capo!)

Tod durch Musen

Something like coasts clover-colored
and in custody of the seas
something like gulls forehead-near and screaming like endured
    destiny
something like historical night monastically brown and burned
    out in the hollows of the island
something like hemp surging genuflexion among the beautiful
    peacocks (shawm)
something like air-wings dream-hedges foam-thicket
something like crystalline kisses night-eye reveling funeral-birds
    (poppy)
something like thin morning in early November
something like rain on sadly-crowned fish (smoke)
something like ashes anxious and whirled wind-high (crisp
    chimneys)

something like velvet blue-ish and around greetings meandering
   on graves
something like stone tender cushion for the dead (sand upon
   sand)
something like skin (honey-warm pupil of the eye)
something like sweetness at the sight of the thousand seas

Tod durch Musen

The marble the stone-cool the
early-spring-gray magic
the anticipating wing-beating magic has finally touched me.
I can't do anything about it
except yield to it with sinking arms and bursting lids
with futile magic formulas no one has written down.
You have entranced me so powerfully that I no longer know
what name I should give you
whether I may summon you
whether I should send you my smile like a letter
over the hills of the city
over the nocturnal bouquets of the stars
through the bellows of the wind
You have changed me into joyous and made me beaming
and the beautiful earth is stretched with your skin
and your mouth is the mouth of a Roman fountain
in whose flowing blessings I can lay my hand
and your eye the color of which I don't know
(is it honey-yellow or blue like nights in spring?)
has become a porthole in a white ship
a large porthole encircled with sea-roses
and with this white ship we shall sail far . . .

In langsamen Blitzen

Wherever you go
with your dreaming feet
carefully set down in your present life
yet strangely-winged like Mercury's heels
in anticipating expectancy:

again and again gigantic blocks of air submissive herds
will let themselves be moved by you

and come toward me
all rain that ever touches your cheek
will come back to me
you are dissolved in every little part of the earth
you have imparted yourself to all hovering clouds
and the forests of flowers speak in your language

nothing can separate you any more from my heart
with each sunbeam you penetrate me
like a sperm

away over all water

up to the leafing stars of the rhumb-card

In langsamen Blitzen

Sometimes in some chance
motion
my hand brushes against your hand the back of your hand
or my body fully clothed leans almost without knowing it
for a moment against your clothed body
these tiniest nearly plant-like motions—
your declining look and your eye intentionally shifting in the
    emptiness
your self-interrupted question where are you going this summer
what are you reading now—
go right to the middle of my heart
and through my throat like a sweet knife
and I dry up like a spring in hot summer

Tod durch Musen

From the Depths

With this overload sweet and tough-hearted like flowers
(a lonely drop of water in the black well of hovering clouds
a silky monster procession of straight-lined sunny ants
an endless street at night
a strange greeting above amber-asking animal eyes

The notched stones of Stonehenge endure violence
a horrible rattling field of intractable stone armies

horizontal-heavy preserve
hard squares of air

Sunk like water pale-blue an imagined paradise enclosed
a swimming gray paradise supported by clouds
yet surrendered: to the summoning depths
the fish-blue canals the confusing footpaths and cat-bridges
the morning twilights) mourned crowned. .

Tod durch Musen

The yew trees in ice:
walls of lost singers black in blue
the sharp intrusion of winter stiff in puddles
hedges of necromancy hedges transformation hedges moon-
    brush
sun or moon (something awful is on the way)
the yew trees have turned—
on the death-road Monza as the trees were removed
lombardian trees with black lightning
the violet halberds of the sun
crossed in front of their frozen shadows

the sky-blocks of tear-poplars weeping-willows life-trees
funnel-shaped
beautiful heads
hovering over the edges of streets
spirit-feet something above the concrete

ochre-grasses harp-flowers wounded soft-parts of Monza
horizons hammer ragingly down

Tod durch Musen

The squadron-blue the hemp-yellow drink
of triumph
passed from sun to sun in the blooming breezes
from moon to moon beloved departed face
always on ahead over twilight gables October Sunday
into the mountains thundering with rainbow-colored feet
chestnut-pushing withered wood
driven from gate to gate nail-splitting and cracked centenary

monumental beech trees turned toward themselves and
   compressed
grown over a hundred winters and awakened by a hundred
   springs
from gate to gate in the fog the rebounding drops
between the graves like gardens inexpressibly sad
from thoughts and desire to return and November-flowers
(plant pansies with a shovel in the middle of the grave) and
bending from star to star and from bridge to bridge

Tod durch Musen

Crouched in the chirping
   of your seven-colored ear
I call you master of flute-playing
   god of the salt!

and the fauna of winter black-fingered against the window
   crusted in feathered crystal. .

Master of flute-playing! God of the salt!
   white-shady in vows of the flowers
      in cross-tones and lost starts
         like Socrates!

with agitated flight into the stiffness of day
   you seek softness!
   Do you strive for the steadfastness of rich lines?
   for the melancholy of starry veins?

stone-checkered missing forever: pineal of the flesh!

. . truly in delusions; in beaming measures; in metal-eyed
   houses tight from stretched time; in
      tentacles of inflated philosophies; in
         Hölderlin; in the colonial style of the heart!

(. . traces of Flamenco
   in the scent of your blondness:
      rose!

   . . "my way is flight" . .)

deposed from the capital of scented authorities;
   lost on the thin-threadedness of drawn-out discussions;
      barking in feuds of unfathomable land-paths;

with measured step; morning-clear;

monumental:

in the water-gorge of two American harps (Ravel):

    :a collection of small Swabian bushes
    :all songs of Greece
    :the green frozen gutters of knowledge

Tod durch Musen

(model 3 / melpomene):

enticed into rhine-mine-snare; the raging one
drawn in; held high; hanged; with the hind end up;
sunk—
outcry of total pain (sound brought forth with lips pressed
    together)

(poet.) explosion; snuff of the lampwick / roar
raging with wine
unchained woman!
and already we are in the midst of the suspicious abstraction

Tod durch Musen

Oceanic World

toward morning
an impatient, breathless
rapacious
dreaming:
the desire
for a quick awakening
brief arising
falling asleep again immediately
without having to turn on the light

(under water the source /
under cover)

on the moon-lit
windowsill the pale
frozen roses

Gute Nacht, guten Morgen

Cypress

the wind
blows white, the
bird
clatters in the
wood—
embracing
tender strangeness when
the blossom
withers

Gute Nacht, guten Morgen

Numbness

unlovely place
unlovely association
with myself, waiting
for some kind of promise:
postman telephone
direction of the moon
color of the sky
act of nature / hedge-
headed rose-color

several times a day the clock (the alarm)
this split-up time! turned
toward any, the nearest
benevolence

finally the last
sun gilded at the side
of the ear
comforting, and glowing with wax of idle
rose

Gute Nacht, guten Morgen

After reading the poetry
of Yannis Ritsos

now, I think, finally
I am far enough
so I can call
them all to me
without making a sound:
finally, I think, now,
without having to make
self-reproach, now, I think,
finally, I have stopped
pursuing myself.

Gute Nacht, guten Morgen

[Translator's note: Born in 1909 in Laconia, Yannis Ritsos is one of the leading poets in Greece today. His works have been translated throughout the world, particularly in Europe and the United States.]

KARL WAWRA

Karl Wawra (1924–   ) lives in Vienna, where, following a youthful career as actor, he works in industry. His prose and poetry demonstrate a subtle sense of humor, treading a fine line between depth and play, ceding to neither pathos nor cynicism. Several volumes of poetry written exclusively in rhyme and meter could not be represented here; the free-verse selections below are from *Die Auferstehung der Sonnenblume* (Wien: Bergland, 1968).

The Scarecrow in Capri

She stands under the white sun
in the sirocco
wearing an old fur coat,
the deserted villa of moths,
and the hat of a tourist
from perhaps 1920,
and farm coveralls
that never fit very well,
with a scarf
whose knot must be admired.
She doesn't move much
under the white sun
in the sirocco.

She has underwear of straw
that shows here and there
but only a little.

Her face must be very beautiful,
for she carefully conceals it
so as not to be stared at,
or she fears for her complexion
under the white sun
in the sirocco,
or she's bashful.

All day long
she doesn't move much
in the sirocco
under the white sun;
because the sun becomes white
in the sirocco
she doesn't move much
the whole day.

She pays no attention
to the grapes, the birds.
The calls of the tower clock
she ignores, like the
monologue of the hens,
the murmur of the sea,
the cock's crow.
She doesn't bother about
olive tree, oak, and fern,
doesn't even hear the lizards,
the cats and the dog.

But in the evening
at the elegant hour
after dinner, long after the
white sun in the sirocco has set,
she goes off to the piazza.

She goes in her fur coat
with her face covered,
past the many faces,
and she moves speechlessly
among the many languages
that mix indiscriminately,
and in many dialects
people ask: Who's that?
When she,
with her face concealed
like the white sun
in the sirocco,
slowly and strangely
crosses the piazza.

Die Auferstehung der Sonnenblume

Capri as Cloud

You're there again?
You've stretched
yourself out
grayly
across the evening sky,
the Tyrrhenian Sea.
The night
moves broadly
toward you.
Behind you is the
sun, the big
emerald, and later
stars spring up
from you.
Stay,
beautiful chimera.

Die Auferstehung der Sonnenblume

Antique Shop in New York

Among the things
from old Europe
that don't speak,
simply are,
the wonderful chair
and St. Ildefonso;
the enchanting shopkeeper
revealed to his
transient guest
the secret.

We thanked him for it.
We too said something
in the same
speechless language
of a similar
smile.

Die Auferstehung der Sonnenblume

ALOIS HERGOUTH

Alois Hergouth (1925–   ) is a native of Graz, where he taught folklore at the university for many years. His poetry reflects a sense of realism and often expresses mild social criticism. Translations are from *Schwarzer Tribut* (Graz: Leykam, 1958) and *Flucht zu Odysseus* (Graz: Styria, 1975).

The Fall

The picture book torn,
scraps of paper
washed by the rain;
the doll clothes
with ragged arms.

No window, as before.
No step
through the shadow in the rear.

The sandman in exile.

The magic formula forgotten,
the flower petrified
the light in the glass ball.

Schwarzer Tribut

Interim Balance

It would be too easy
simply to draw a line,
to say: that's the sum.
One doesn't close the account that way.
The number of bottles we drank,
the number of movies and cigarettes—
that's no result.

Too easily said:
That's over; and
tomorrow is another day.
For tomorrow is never
or only when it's today.
And the day after tomorrow
is already yesterday.
Even when we bathe,
change our clothes and shoes,
we carry it with us.

What is forgetting?
When is it over?
Is there a file without contents,
a big wastepaper basket of the soul?
Where is the past?
Did it go to the moon?
One doesn't get any farther
with old calendars and diaries.

What will be and what was
is the same in the end.
But each second
passes through us directly
and is real
and transforms the world.

Schwarzer Tribut

Venetian Fragment

The moon splashes
in the green canals.
A moon for travel agencies,
for lovers

from Vienna and Paris.
Silver moon,
Golden moon—
like sparkling coins
strewn on the water.
Gondola-moon
on the rocking masts
of the boats.

But the sea
beyond the quay
is dark.
And the night
remains the same.

And above,
the other city
in the large, strange lagoon
goes by slowly,
very slowly.

Flucht zu Odysseus

Farewell

It will be hard
to go so suddenly,
perhaps in the middle of the day
or in the evening
before the concert begins.
The tea will still be warm,
the bed.
And the book on the table
not yet finished. . .

One doesn't believe it:
but still,
it was always that way.

The whistle at the train station:
Don't sleep any longer! Be careful!
The signal
at the intersection.
And suddenly a rush

five minutes
before departure.

But perhaps
it won't be so hard.
Perhaps only a step,
only a moment
on the threshold—
that which one leaves
before stepping out
into freedom.

Schwarzer Tribut

ERNST JANDL

Ernst Jandl (1925–   ) is a leading exponent of "concrete poetry." Singly, as well as in collaboration with Friederike Mayröcker, he is among the most prominent Austrian authors writing today. Bristling with intellect, irritation, and surprise, his long list of publications includes the following volumes, from which selections were taken: *Laut und Luise* (1966) and *Sprechblasen* (1968; both reprinted at Stuttgart: Reclam, 1976 and 1979); *Der künstliche Baum* (1970), *dingfest* (1973), and the collection *für alle* (1974), all three at Darmstadt: Luchterhand.

From "Statements and Peppermints": Austrian Contributions to a Modern World Poetry*

1. The goal of a growing number of contemporary poets is to devise new methods of writing according to which new kinds of language constructs can be produced. The movement in its European form was initiated in the 1950s by the Swiss poet Eugen Gomringer, and it has since become intercontinental in scope. "Concrete" or "experimental" are the appellations most frequently applied to this type of literature.

2. This modern world poetry, in its purest form, is a poetry that does not distract from itself, that does not lead one to think of other things. It is not

---

*[Translator's note: Abridged and renumbered at the suggestion of the author.]

illusionistic and is not didactic. It is a poetry that contains nothing one can "know."

3. It is "concrete" in that it materializes possibilities latent within the language and produces objects from language itself (instead of making statements, didactic and abstract, about objects assumed outside of language; or offering linguistic imitations, illusionistic and abstract, of the realization of possibilities assumed outside of language).

4. This poetry is measurable neither on a world conceived apart from language nor on the conventions of a language whose purpose is practical communication.

5. It is a poetry that establishes closed systems of relations. It does not force any connection with an external reality because it is itself a part of this external reality—not a voice speaking from one inner world to another inner world about an outer world.

6. Contact with such poetry—in looking, reading, hearing—is a passing by, as with paintings, a touching of the surface. It knows no depth, perspective, or three-dimensionality, and neither does it attempt to simulate such. It doesn't feign anything. It makes clear. It makes surfaces clear. Like painting, it is—solely—flatness, surface area. From the encounter with it there remains only the recollection of words, sequences, surfaces. In regard to knowledge, there remains only this: to have seen, read, heard something definite; and, in regard to possibility, only this: to repeat the event of encounter, the brushing of a surface area.

7. It is a poetry of pure consciousness, of disengaged intellect, which is a prerequisite for its reception, as well as an effect of the encounter with it. It is like absolute music, which, to be truly perceived, likewise requires an emptiness of mind; the music passes through the mind during the period of its duration, and, if it is strong enough and if the receiver is willing, it continues to work for a while after it has stopped, rendering the receiver immune to other sensations that may press in from the outside.

8. Art today, thus also poetry, can be interpreted as a continual realization of freedom.

für alle

woman at the window

the elbow-queen on the windowsill
eats in the evening with her granary-eyes
all the corn-ripe young ladies
on the stretch of street under her control

she threshes them out and finds nothing but
black kernels, unpalatable even for the pigeons
that she graciously feeds on the windowsill
in the morning.

für alle

four attempts at definition

love
is the hurt at being separated from you

love
is the joy at being together with you

love
is the recitation of unimportant words in your presence

love
is the occasional non-believer in me

für alle

travelogue

i went one night
from vienna to paris
without taking leave
of myself.

as i got off the train in paris
i was already there
to shake my hand.

as i got off
the train in london

i ran behind
and jumped on my back.

the taxi driver
had his misgivings
i had to bow
unusually low.

since then i sit
across from myself
just as one sits
at a dull tea party.

we pass the time
by writing letters
home together
to me and myself and i.

für alle

jupiter	uninhabited
mercury	uninhabited
saturn	uninhabited
uranus	uninhabited
neptune	uninhabited
venus	uninhabited
pluto	uninhabited
mars	uninhabited
earth	uninhabitable

für alle

BIOGRAPHY

for Ian Hamilton Finlay

```
d     eat     h
 d    eat    h
  d   eat   h
   d eat h
   death

COMING ...

    earth
     e art h
     e   art   h
     e   art    h
    e    art      h

... AND GOING

    e      art.    h
     e     art    h
      e    art   h
       e art h
       earth

       SHIP

       scratch
        sc rat ch
       sc   rat   ch
      sc    rat    ch
     sc     rat     ch

     h     ear    t
      h    ear    t
       h   ear  t
        h ear t
        heart
```

[Translator's note: This poem was written originally in English.]

LIFEBOAT

```
    drown
   d row n
  d  row  n
 d   row    n
d    row     n
```

STEPS

```
p    lane    t
 p   lane   t
  p  lane  t
   p lane t
    planet
```

MEADOW PEACE

```
   clover
  c love r
 c  love  r
c   love   r
c   love    r
```

I AM

```
a    i    m
 a   i   m
  a  i  m
   a i m
    aim
```

```
   just
  j us t
 j  us  t
j   us   t
j    us    t
```

THE POSSESSED GIRL

```
h    i    s
 h   i   s
  h  i  s
   h i s
    his
```

WEATHER OR NOT

```
         born
       b  or  n
        b    or    n
      b      or      n
    b       or        n


      s     no     w
       s     no    w
         s   no   w
          s no w
            snow


          glide
        g  lid  e
       g    lid    e
      g     lid      e
     g      lid         e
```

POOR. OLD. TIRED. HORSE.

```
     t      rut       h
      t      rut      h
        t   rut   h
         t rut h
           truth


          joke
        j  ok  e
       j    ok    e
      j      ok      e
     j       ok         e
```

TESTAMENT

```
    c      and       y
     c      and     y
       c   and   y
        c and y
          candy
```

Der künstliche Baum

verdict

this man's poems are unusable.

first
i rubbed one on my bald spot.
in vain. it didn't promote growth of hair.

then
i used one to dab my pimple. within two days
it reached the size of a medium potato.
the doctors were amazed.

then
i broke two into the frying pan.
somewhat suspicious, i didn't eat them myself.
my dog died of them.

then
i used one as a condom.
consequently i paid for the abortion.

then
i clamped one on my eye
and entered one of the better clubs.
the doorman
stuck out his foot to trip me.

thereupon
i passed the above-mentioned verdict.

dingfest

on rainy shadows

"i instinctively
reject
certain things"
is the death
of many of our debates.
thus i untiringly extend
the discussion of subjects such as
are communists human, does
man want change, or is friendship
with the divorced spouse to be recommended
to great lengths until the topic
becomes decisive, like the telegraph wire

with which henri rousseau neutralized
the raspberry taste of the idyllic landscape.
at the end of such debates
i usually lean
like a beam of light through unyielding clouds
cross-wise on rainy shadows.
the sun has no instincts.
i long for
clear days.

dingfest

on the life of trees

even the hard black
buds, even the late
buds are opened by light.

even the beautiful white
blossoms, even the fragrant
blossoms are scattered by the wind.

even the beautiful green
leaves, even the bright sunny
leaves are ground down by the wind.

even the big old
trees, even the faithful
trees are broken by time.

dingfest

lying, with you

I lie with you. your arms
hold me. your arms
hold more than I am.
your arms hold what I am
when I lie with you and
your arms hold me.

dingfest

pockets

look, so many pockets.
in this one I keep postcards.

in this one two watches,
my time and your time.

in this one a die.
23 eyes see more than two.

you can imagine
how many spectacles I drag around.

dingfest

forenoons

by the four-storied tower of a middle school
a forenoon goes by like two people
under one umbrella who have suddenly
always gotten along well.

but it can't rain forever. (besides
the afternoon is yet to come.)

the other forenoon does not go by
but puts ladders at the windows to the east,
climbs up the ladders, goes in through the windows
(I am an ambassador—I am a mechanic)
and installs a piece of sunshine
on each bench
and slowly turns the window-bars
from west to north.

(then when noon fumes from the soup
it is already almost evening.)

dingfest

dilection

some think
reft and light
cannot be
leversed
what an
irrusion.

Laut und Luise

figure of speech

i'll
break
you
yet

deardaddypleasebendmeinstead

Sprechblasen

perfection

e
ee
eei
eeio

p
pr
prf
prfc
prfct
prfctn

ep
eepr
eeiprf
eeioprfc
eeioprfct
eeioprfctn

pe
pree
prfeei
prfceeio
prfcteeio
prfctneeio

prfcteneio
prfcetneio
prfectneio
prefctneio
perfctneio

perfctenio
perfcetnio
perfectnio

perfectio
perfection

Sprechblasen

INGEBORG BACHMANN

Ingeborg Bachmann (1926–73) won international fame as one of the leading poets of the Austrian and German postwar period. The existential themes of temporality and consciousness, as well as a concern for language and the creative process, find expression in her evocative imagery and spell-binding rhythms. She also wrote prose and radio plays, but her talent was primarily lyrical. The two well-known poetry volumes, *Die gestundete Zeit* (1953) and *Anrufung des Großen Bären* (1956), have been collected in *Werke, I* (1978), all at München: Piper.

Psalm

1

Be silent with me, as all bells are silent!

In the aftermath of horror
the vermin look for new nourishment.
For display on Good Fridays a hand hangs
on the firmament, two fingers are missing;
it cannot swear that everything,
everything did not really happen and that nothing
will happen. It plunges into the redness of clouds,
escapes the new murderers
and goes free.

At night on this earth
reaching through windows, throwing back the covers

so the secrecy of the sick one is exposed,
an abscess full of nourishment, endless pain
for any taste.

The butchers with gloves on
stop the breath of the exposed one,
the moon in the doorway falls to the floor,
let the pieces lie, the handle. . .

Everything was prepared for extreme unction.
(The sacrament cannot be consummated.)

2

How futile it all is.
Roll out a city,
raise yourself from the dust of that city,
assume a position
and disguise yourself
to avoid exposure.

Redeem a promise
in front of a blind mirror in the air,
in front of a closed door in the wind.

The paths are untraveled on the steep wall of heaven.

3

O eyes, burned by the sun's storehouse earth,
burdened with the rain-load of all eyes,
and now tightly spun, woven shut
by the tragic spiders
of the present. . .

4

Place a word
in the trough of my muteness
and raise forests on both sides
so that my mouth lies
completely in shadow.

Die gestundete Zeit

Theme and Variations

The honey combs did not produce that year.
The queen bees took their swarms and flew away,
Strawberry patches dried up overnight,
The workers went home early in dismay.

A beam of light transported all that sweetness
into a sleep. Who slept before the time?
Honey and berries? Happy is the person,
who has it all, and all things in their prime.

And nothing is missing, only a little,
to be able to rest or to stand up straight.
Caves bent him down and shadows,
for no country permitted him to enter.
Even in the mountains he was not safe
—a partisan whom the world handed over
to its dead companion, the moon.

Happy is the person who has everything,
and what doesn't he have? The cohorts
of beetles fought in his hand, fires
heaped up scars on his face and the oasis
appeared as chimera before his eyes
where it was not.

Honey and berries?
Had he known the smell, he would have followed it long ago!

Somnambulistic sleep while he was walking,
who slept before the time?
One who was born old
and had to go early into the darkness.
A beam of light transported all that sweetness
past him.

He spewed the curse that brings drought
into the underbrush, he howled
and was heard:
the workers went home early!
As the root arose
and glided whistling after them,
a snake skin remained as the tree's last protection.
Strawberry patches dried up over night.

Down in the village the pails stood empty
and drum-ready in the yards.
Thus the sun struck
and whirled the death.

The windows fell shut,
the queen bees took their swarms and flew away,
and no one hindered them in their departure.
The wilderness received them,
the hollow tree in the ferns
absorbed the first free country.
The last man was pierced
by a thorn without pain.

The honey combs did not produce that year.

Die gestundete Zeit

Fogland

In winter my beloved is
among the beasts of the forest.
The vixen knows that I must return
before morning and laughs.
How the clouds tremble! And
a coat of cracked ice
falls on my snow collar.

In winter my beloved is
a tree among trees and invites
the lonely crows in to her
beautiful branches. She knows
that at dawn the wind will lift
her hoar-frosted evening
gown and chase me home.

In winter my beloved is
mute and among the fish.
Bound to the waters that are stirred
from within by the stroke of her fins,
I stand on the shore and watch
how she dives and turns
till the ice floes drive me away.

And struck again by the hunting call
of the bird that stiffens its wings
above me, I fall
on the open field: she defeathers
the hens and throws me a white
collarbone. I hang it around my neck
and go off through the bitter down.

My beloved is faithless.
I know that sometimes she soars
in high heels to the city,
in bars she kisses the mouths
of the glasses deeply with straws,
and she finds words for everyone.
But I don't understand that language.

I have seen fog land.
I have eaten fog heart.

Anrufung des Grossen Bären

To the Sun

More beautiful than the notable moon and its ennobled light,
more beautiful than the stars, the celebrated orders of night,
much more beautiful than the fiery course of a comet,
and appointed to a far more beautiful position than any other
    celestial body,
because your life and mine depend on it every day, is the sun.

Beautiful sun that rises, not forgetting its task,
and sets, most beautifully in summer, when a day
evaporates on the coast and draws the sails, freely reflected,
past your eyes until you get tired and foreshorten it.

Without the sun even art would reassume its veil.
You don't appear to me any more, and the sea and the sand,
scourged by shadows, flee under my eyelids.

Beautiful light that keeps us warm, preserves and wondrously
    provides
that I see again and see you again!

Nothing more beautiful under the sun than to be under the
    sun. . .

Nothing more beautiful than to see the stick in the water and the
    bird above
that ponders its flight and the fish in shoals below.

Colored, formed, come into the world with a mission of light,
and to see the expanse, the square of a field, the thousand corners
    of my country,
and the dress that attires you; and your dress, bell-shaped and
    blue!

Beautiful blue in which peacocks strut and bow,
blue of the distances, the zones of happiness with climates that
    match my moods,
blue contingency on the horizon! And my enraptured eyes
widen again and then blink and burn themselves sore.

Beautiful sun that even from dust deserves great admiration.
Therefore, not because of the moon and the stars and not
because the night parades with its comets and seeks a dupe in me,
but for your sake and almost interminably and as for nothing else,
I shall bewail the irrevocable loss of my eyesight.

                                           Anrufung des grossen Bären

My Bird

Regardless: the devastated world
sinks back into twilight,
the woods hold ready a sleeping potion,
and from the tower that the watchman abandoned
the eyes of the owl look calmly and steadily down.

Regardless: you know the right time,
my bird, you take your veil
and fly through the fog to me.

We stare through the haze that the rabble inhabits.
You follow my nod, you thrust out
and whirl your plumage and pelt—

My ice-gray shoulder companion, my weapon,
armed with that feather, my only weapon!
My only adornment: veil and feather from you.

Even if my skin burns
in the needle-dance under the tree
and the hip-high bush
tempts me with spicy leaves,
when a lock of my hair shoots up,
shakes, and is consumed,
then the refuse of stars pours down
precisely on my hair.

When I, helmeted with smoke,
again know what happened,
my bird, my stay of the night,

when I am inflamed in the night,
it crackles in the dark residue,
and I drive out the spark.

When I remain as I am ablaze
and loved by the fire
until the resin pours out of its shaft,
dresses the wounds, and warmly
enwraps the earth,
(and even if you divest my heart of the night,
my bird of faith and my bird of fidelity!)
that watchtower will come to light
to which you, placated,
fly in serene repose—
regardless.

Anrufung des Grossen Bären

Word and Afterword

Don't come forth from our mouth,
Word that sows the dragon.
It's true, the air is sultry;
fermented and soured, the light foams up,
and over the swamp hangs a dark swarm of flies.

The hemlock tipples too much.
A cat skin is on display,
the snake hisses,
the scorpion begins to dance.

Don't come to our ears,
rumor of other guilt;
Word, die in the swamp
whence the mud pool arises.

Word, be with us
in gentle patience
and impatience. This sowing
must come to an end!

One does not approach an animal by imitating animal sounds.
He who surrenders the secret of his bed forfeits all love.
The word's bastard is good for a joke to sacrifice a fool.

Who asked you to judge this stranger? And if you do so

unasked, you must go around from night to night
with his sores on your feet, go! don't come back.

Word, be of us,
free-minded, clear, beautiful.
There must indeed be an end
to precautions.

(The crayfish retreats,
the mole oversleeps,
the soft water dissolves
the lime that spun stones.)

Come, favor of sound and breath,
strengthen this mouth
when its weakness
horrifies and hinders us.

Come and don't fail,
since we are at war with so much wrong.
Before dragon blood protects the enemy
this hand will pass through the fire.
My Word, deliver me!

Anrufung des Grossen Bären

Go on, Idea

Go on, Idea, clear for flight, since a Word
is your wing, lifts you up and flies to the place
where the light metals sway,
where the air is pierced
with a new understanding,
where weapons speak
of a peerless way.
Defend us there!

The wave brought up driftwood and sinks.
The fever seized hold of you, lets you fall.
Only one mountain has been moved by faith.

What is, let be, go on, Idea!,

permeated by nothing other than our pain.
Be commensurate with us completely!

Werke

Prague, January 1964

Since that night
I walk again and I speak,
it sounds Bohemian,
as if I were back home,

where between the Vltava, the Danube,
and my childhood river
everything has a conception of me.

Going, it came back step by step,
Seeing, looked upon, I learned again.

Still stooped, blinking,
I stood at the window,
saw the shadow years,
in which no star
hung in my mouth,
recede in the distance.

Above the Hradschin
at six in the morning
with their torn claws
the snow shovelers from the Tartary
removed the chunks of ice-cover.

Under the bursting blocks
of my—also of my—river
the pent-up waters flowed forth.

To be heard as far as the Urals.

Werke

Days in White

These days I get up with the birches
and comb the wheat-hair from my forehead
in front of a mirror of ice.

Mixed with my breath,
the milk thickens.
It foams easily this early.
And when I breathe on the window, your name,
painted by a childlike finger,

appears again: innocence!
After such a long time.

These days it doesn't bother me
that I can forget
and must remind myself.

I love. To the point of passion
I love and thank with an Ave Maria.
I learned it in flight.

These days I think of the albatross
with which I soared
up and over
to an undescribed country.

There on the horizon I see,
splendid in its demise,
my fabulous continent,
which discharged me
in a shroud.

I live and hear from a distance its swan song!

Anrufung des Grossen Bären

A Kind of Loss

Used jointly: seasons, books, and music.
The keys, the tea cups, the bread basket, linen sheets, and a bed.
A dowry of words, of gestures, brought along, used, used up.
A domestic routine. Said. Done. And the hand always extended.

With winter, a Viennese septet, and with summer I fell in love.
With road maps, a mountain village, a beach, and a bed.
Formed a cult with the calendar, declared promises binding,
idolized Something and was pious in the presence of Nothing,

(—the folded newspaper, the cold ashes, the note with a memo)
fearless in religion, for this bed was the church.

From the seascape emerged my inexhaustible painting.
From the balcony the people, my neighbors, were greeted.
By the open fire, secure, my hair reached its utmost color.
The ring of the doorbell was the alarm for my joy.

Not you have I lost,
but the world.

Werke

KLAUS DEMUS

Klaus Demus (1927–   ), as art historian and archeologist, has a keen sense
of spatial form. Landscapes assume mythic dimensions in his poems, which
hymnically evoke other levels both above and below the panoramic vistas.
Selections are from *Die Morgennacht* (1969), *Das Morgenleuchten* (1979),
and *Schatten vom Wald* (1983), all at Pfullingen: Neske.

Summer Report

The far, thundering days
the former time in the forest,
the paths, wrought
in the hard waste of the mountains,
in the dark blows of the storms.
Early mornings, quiet
in fog and rain
in the narrow valley, and
sometimes, though briefly,
a beam of light breaking through
on the evening gate, insight
offered into the promises, but only
at great distance, before the
closing of the sky.
No high star-gleam at night,
at times the moon, for
a moment, not entirely
swallowed by clouds,
the lake shimmering slightly.

Not much summer. No sort of
summit scaled, only the graying
glaciers, the dully darkened
gorges, in a storm, deep
in snow.

Enough. The year
still has strength for higher
and clearer days. The light
must first become shorter,
changeless, more infinite,
standing then far into the autumn
on the mountains shining
more and more alone.

Das Morgenleuchten

Morning Stillness

Morning stillness.
The peaks and the fog
in a sleeping embrace.
The valleys covered over.
An early, soft light.
The sky is still empty.
The day is open. Everything
is yet to come.

When the sun comes out,
the fog-sea will stir,
fume slowly up the valley
to the peaks;
the predetermined battle
will unfold itself
hugely in the heights.

There is still
time. Premonitions
are still free. The light
is mild and clear, and the law
lies dreaming far off
on half-awakened,
half-concealed
mountains.

Das Morgenleuchten

Steeply upward, the forest.
Fir, rock. Soon
snow. Cloud-near wilderness.
Hollow, gap, ridge. And the
glacier blinding.

Wasteland. Chain
of peaks, wintry.
Gray in the storm-light dark
depths. Then, before evening,
fog. Nightfall. Alone.

Morgennacht

Oh brother, sister—man:
it is the moon
that shines from your eyes;
you look and speak
from her light.
A twilight-waking trust
had built up around us.
I find the deepest right of your words
reflected on the stand of dark woods
and know your breath
far off on the gray glow of the mountains.
The moon gives a dark light:
its lightning fills the nearness, almost a fire,
and yet it remains night; on dark masses
a thin sheen is deceptive.
It doesn't choose your speaking
for concealment:
Long since freed by gazing up at the celestial body,
your looking upward has carried you up
to the shadowless goal, and you say
of the lighting there
in everything what you say.
I, more earthly a being, see, while outwardly
protecting your speaking, stretches of earth
grown over slowly by brilliance, not to be trod on,
wherein the farthest thing, helplessly blossomed out
to purest loneliness, is near to me.
The entire abyss, by which the moon with her light
keeps us apart one from another, unites us.

Schatten vom Wald

KURT KLINGER

Kurt Klinger (1928–   ) takes a position at once traditional and critical, as evidenced by his poetry, which is both rhetorical and skeptical, baroque as well as satiric. He is also known as a dramatist, critic, editor, and director of the Austrian Society for Literature. Selections are from *Löwenköpfe* (Baden: Grasl, 1977), partially reprinted in *Auf dem Limes* (Salzburg: O. Müller, 1980).

We Think Farewell

Leaning back, smoking, without a word.
We could thus look past each other for years.
Each one thinks: Maybe it is already decided.
Maybe, if I don't breathe, it can still be kept open.
Each one thinks: Are you really as sincere as you say?
I believe you—and believe nothing from you. Where is the
    evidence?
I saw happiness in your face, that makes you suspicious.
Between us there is only the celebration and a memory.
Each one thinks: When love begins to hurt, throw it away.
Yet I am more faithful to you than you will be to me.
Each one thinks: I am stronger than you, for I know the end.
It would be better to go away right now.
For your sake I still search for an easier way.
One last time I am willing to spare you.

Löwenköpfe

Never

Never will I leave you,
if I leave you tomorrow. Never
will I forget you,
I've forgotten you already.
Never will you be in need
as long as I live and you are not in need.
Never will I break my promise
that I never promised. Never
until death will I betray you,
until it becomes daily.
Never will I see you again,
I'll come back. Never
have I truly loved you,
for I love you truly.
Never have you made me happy,
happiness beyond bounds. Never
have you understood my life,
only you understand me. Never.
You can count on me. Never.
I am the rock. Never.
That melts in your hands.

Löwenköpfe

Miracle in Milan

Saturday and nothing.
In all waiting rooms
the yawning of the centuries has broken out.

The skyscrapers stumble in the fog
over unpretentious cathedrals
and break their hundred-storied necks
on hallowed stones.

General strike of the cremated crosses.
With arms spread out
Christ falls burning
into my glass of Campari.
I fish him out unobtrusively:
The moth still seems to be alive.

In the Scala
the dismissed angel choirs practice
the death cry of the spheres.
I saw myself in old German boots
as an unborn child
who lost his feet in the ice.

The Metropolitana opens.
The waiters curse the white cloth
on the tables, spotted with the death sweat
of freezing fountains.

I bequeath my despairing fear
head over heels
to your gracious Black Hand.

Löwenköpfe

Mattina

Lovers already at eight in the morning?
What will it be then at eight in the evening
when the dry leaf of chastity falls from the laurel.
Finally one can again see stems
that grow from the sky to the earth.

Löwenköpfe

Cinema

Finally a free evening,
thought the doorkeeper,
and went to the movies.
When he returned
the bloody vultures from Nevada
were sitting on his head
begging for carrion and feeding place.
No tenant is sure of his life any more.

Löwenköpfe

The Crazy Lady

Here comes a lady who would like to be murdered.
In yearning for the knife
she slept off the happiness.
We will not do her the favor.
Now she's coming by for the third time.
She makes a zigzag pattern with her bicycle,
the blood-spattered bushes in her arms.
We ceremoniously take off our hats for her.

Löwenköpfe

The Cats

Seen through cat eyes, all problems become greater.
The panther tongues are red with morning dew.
The aftertaste pensively gives its paws to the foretaste,
and in the golden eye-slits burns the warning:
We are almost on the track of a solution.

Löwenköpfe

Beginning

I

I must build it,
constructed from doubt and darkness.
A building of words,
there I shall live,
in good rooms,
with a view toward all
sides of truth.

Forget the narrow,
gold-ringed hands of happiness.
Strike the stone!
And discard whatever
splits into riddles.

II

I know that I work
for a far-off day of fulfillment.
That these arches
will meet
to form a gateway
whose height and weight
take my breath away.

Bear out
the ever-recurring anxiety
that the world could disappear
in the midst of smoke
in the midst of ascent to blossoming.

Bear out
the round of the inevitable relation
of forehead and dust.

That will become clearer.
And we won't die
so long as hope finds us
so long as we fear
and feel the finger
that closes our
cold eyes.

Auf dem Limes

HERTHA KRÄFTNER

Hertha Kräftner (1928–51) wrote poetry and prose sketches with an individual lyrical voice and highly emotive imagery. A macabre element in her work foreshadows the suicidal end of her active life. Her work was recently rediscovered and published by O. Breicha and A. Okopenko as *Das Werk* (Eisenstadt: Roetzer, 1977).

Litanies

1

You stony angel over the pain.
Nightly bird with sad wing-beat.
Moon-land in yellow and gray.
Pallor of Aaron's rod.
Violet-colored leaf of an iris.
Wild cry of the gypsy with dried blood on his hands.
Bowl of nettles and blooming grass.
Plaintiff song of begging children.
Moaning death of a mad woman.
Whispering meekness of white-barked birches.
Gentle ruffling of the stream on round-washed stones . . .
Are you all that or the image of love?
I opened my heart up for you,
and the world came confusedly in.

2

I idolize you with litanies:
You, who blow in the wind as passion.
You, taste of peaches on my tongue.
Wandering moon in the big city.
Bat wings, restlessly twitching in the attic darkness.
Sharp smell of almonds and wood.
Knowledge of fear and death in the eye of the hushed raven.
You, luminous blue on the pieces of vase from China.
Curse and howl of a drunken old man.
Intoxicant from wine and white jasmine.
Rosewood-colored ribbon in the hair of the loving girl.
Springing death in the narrow pupil of the quiet cat.
You—bridge between morning and evening.
Sleeping core in the midst of the fruit they call "world."

3

You, pushed-in window in terribly beautiful countries!
Veiled shrine of a yellow god.
Smell of seaweed and tar and violet creepers.
Poison-green juice of more southern plants
that heal madness.
Dark moon on pink-blistered and brown bogs.
Gently-molted zebra, fleeing before black-yellow eyes.
Cloud of desert sand and the last cry of the animals.
Coiling snake under the rug of the temple.
Seething salt vapor on the white-gray lake.
Taste of blood and ivory
in the mouth of the lone man roving primeval forests.
O you window of love in never-seen lands.

Das Werk

Who still believes
that coral reefs await us there,
and birds that sing the secret
and dip their frail beaks
in the rose-colored water
and that we will be met
by the aroma
of slivered almonds
and the white root of rare plants?

Oh, death will smell
like pepper and marjoram
because he's been with the fish dealer
who choked on the silver tail
of a pickled herring.

Das Werk

If one had a Blue Vase and a Clock in an Old Wooden Cabinet

If one had a blue vase
with a gold rim around the edge
and scattered clusters of apple blossoms
painted in white and pink and a bluish green,
if there
where the neck gently bows outward,
the blue became deeper, bluer
(like the sky on the horizon
where there are trees),
then he could tell his beloved:
I brought it from China,
but the girls there
are not so nice as you.

If one had a clock
in an old wooden cabinet
with golden numbers
on the yellowish clockface
and cut-glass doors in front,
a clock that struck every quarter hour
with the sound of the bell
that they ring only
when children have died,
then he couldn't conceal
from his beloved in the morning
that he wanted to be alone.

Das Werk

It is an ocean voyage to you,
since the sea is always there
in front of love
and out at sea only the storm.
Hero's time is still present . . .
My ship has been on the way
for years.
Islands go by,
lighted by the moon,
coasts of sand, sad and empty.
A brown man gives flag-signals
at the pier.
Flutes, snakes, and wine in bars.
And the strong wind.
Wind with the smell of fish and
the cry of the albatross and wind
with the mist of foreign harbors.
The sea and the wind
beat loudly against my boat,
but the helmsman
is a mute oriental.
In whatever way I love you,
you are still an ocean voyage away.
Do you remember
that in Hero's time
the lighthouse always
went out? And God's wind
swells the sails
only slowly.

Das Werk

[Translator's note: Hero was a priestess of Aphrodite beloved by Leander, who nightly swam the Hellespont to visit her; upon finding him drowned, Hero drowned herself.]

RENÉ ALTMANN

René Altmann (1929–78) was a prolific writer of the 1950s and 1960s, and his work exemplifies the new beginnings of Austrian poetry in the postwar period. The most complete edition of his work is a collection, selected by Altmann with the aid of his fellow-poets, F. Mayröcker and A. Okopenko, and published posthumously in the journal *protokolle* 4 (1979).

When Will the Bird Cry Again?

When will the bird cry again?
Look: The City.
Sunlight makes pale houses even paler
The air smells heavy.
Or it rains
To no advantage.

When will the bird cry again?
Not merely sing with small joy in the evening.
But cry.
For crying means New Land.

protokolle

Late Fall

The trees are not made of bluebirds
The wind does not sing in rose-colored moons
The afternoon is not full of golden fruit
The night is not an island of blue velvet

The street does not dream of yellow flowers
The houses are not made of hyacinth
The stars have gone down in the freezing water
The pond is not made of your shoulders

The white blossoms are also tear-stained
And the flames are strangled in wet leaves
The horizon is broken into brown fragments
The gardens are burned in the rain.

protokolle

Impression

Octo-
ber
means
the sun
getting
faster
and cooler
wandering
from tower
to tower

The bird
—quadratic—

protokolle

WIELAND SCHMIED

Wieland Schmied (1929–   ) is a noted art historian as well as a poet, and he is currently Director of the DAAD artists' program in Berlin. Theoretical knowledge, however, is not allowed to intrude on his phenomenological perception of painting and sculpture. Such experiences, as well as actual conversations with artists, form the basis of his poems in the volume illustratively entitled *Schach mit Marcel Duchamp* (Stuttgart: Klett, 1980). Selections are from that volume, and a recent piece is from *Literatur und Kritik* (1982).

Thinking of Constantin Brancusi

In the summer of 1945,
thinking of Brancusi,
Ezra Pound,
imprisoned
in a death cell
at the Camp in Pisa,
imagined
the soaring form
of the bird
cut from
"Cavity in
the Pine Tree"
and thought
for a moment
that a breath of air
had touched him.

226

In November of 1972,
thinking
of Pound's
Pisan Cantos,
I saw
Brancusi's bird
leave
its pedestal
in the museum,
as if there were
no prison
that could hold it.

Schach mit Marcel Duchamp

[Translator's note: This poem probably alludes to Pound's notes for Canto CXVIII, which begins as follows: "For the blue flash and the moments / benedetta / the young for the old / that is tragedy / And for one beautiful day there was peace. / Brancusi's bird / in the hollow of pine trunks / or when the snow was like sea foam / Twilit sky leaded with elm boughs."]

Meeting with Giorgio de Chirico

After I left the building
at the Spanish Steps last night
and came back to the Hotel Inghilterra,
I tried to reproduce
the strange perspective
I had seen
in de Chirico's
Piazza d'Italia.
Without difficulty my pen
sketched the architecture,
the towers and their shadows;
the arcades lined up
by themselves.
But the lines met,
as usual,
all in one point,
and the secret,
to which I had felt so close,
remained impenetrable.

Schach mit Marcel Duchamp

Opinions about the Painter de Chirico

Apollinaire thought
he had
viewed things
as if they didn't exist,
a metaphysician
of painting

Cocteau thought
he had
created a cosmos
from the shadows of the arcades,
a classicist
out of yearning

Breton thought
he had
been untrue to himself
when he was influenced by Titian,
a betrayer
of his dreams

Max Ernst thought
he had
only then achieved his goal
when he repudiated his best works,
a Dadaist
against his will

He himself thought
he had
never changed
and denied
ever having been any different
than he was at present

The critical derision
that accompanied his work
for seventy years
always reminded him
of the indisputability
of his identity

Schach mit Marcel Duchamp

The Things of René Magritte

You said:
This is not an apple
and painted
it so large
that it filled the whole room

You said:
this is not a rose
and painted
it like stone
so that it would never fade

You said:
this is not a moon
and painted
it three times in the night-sky
so that it appeared even to the neighbors

Again and again
you had to say,
this is *not an apple, not a rose, not a moon.*
Your contemporaries, unaccustomed to images,
would otherwise not have seen them.

Schach mit Marcel Duchamp

Max Ernst's Walk

Max Ernst
who had to forgo his evening walk
because of the rainy weather
in Normandy
discovered
while observing
the boards in the floor of his hotel
something
between the planks
of the worn-out timber-work
that seemed
like the crescent
of a moon
and he thus found himself
unexpectedly

in the company of
Caspar David Friedrich

                                              Schach mit Marcel Duchamp

Francis Bacon paints Velázquez's Pope

Innocent X
is said to have
hesitated a long time
before sitting for Bacon

Popes have never
thought much
of artists

The order
of the Inquisition
lay nearer
their hearts

In this regard
not much has changed
in two thousand years

Thus he came
in purple or violet
in order
to represent

But when he saw
the world
the painter
revealed to him

he began to scream

He recognized it
as *His* work.

                                              Schach mit Marcel Duchamp

With Giorgio Morandi in Bologna

You never left Bologna
    always stayed with your objects
        pitcher and pot   vase and glass
            and the dusty bottles in the studio

Your whole life as teacher
    in the craft of etching
        to teach Art
            didn't seem possible

With an eye for small objects
    you always painted the same
        in the soft light of
            a gray   a brown   an ochre

Thinking of Bologna
    we remember these colors
        as if it were possible
            to breathe *light*

                                    Schach mit Marcel Duchamp

Mark Tobey's Legacy

At his estate
in St. Alban near Basel
was found, among the many
papers, sketches, and scrawlings,
a tea-stained note
on which only two words
were legible:
"no tragic."

They thought
it must have concerned
something private
and put it aside
with the old train tickets,
dried leaves and grasses,
things that were of no significance
for the appraisal of the estate.

Only the secretary,
who had served the house for a long time,
wanted to keep it;
he felt
it concerned
Tobey's legacy.
But he hesitated
to say anything.

Schach mit Marcel Duchamp

Remembrances of Guernica

Picasso didn't want to paint Guernica
the name meant little to him
What did he know about that place
in the heart of Basque territory?
It was they who tried to destroy it
it was their planes that darkened the sky
their bombs that devastated the earth
It was they who wrote the name on his consciousness
until it pursued him day and night
until it horrified him awake and asleep
until he began to draw:
the shriek from the mouth of a horse
the rage in the nostrils of a bull
the agony in the eyes of a people
until Guernica became a word
for dismembered bodies, defiled creatures, eclipsed light.
That can no longer be separated,
it belongs together as from the beginning of time:
as long as there are paintings   .
they will tell what people do to each other,
and as long as injustice prevails,
there will also be art
so that we never get used to it.

Literatur und Kritik

In Memory of Reinhold Koehler

to destroy in order to perceive
to destroy in order to discover

to destroy in order to understand
to destroy in order to test

to destroy in order to see
in order to see the change
to see the destroyed
the destruction
                         to see the other
              in order to see at all
to destroy in order to see

to destroy in order to take apart
in order to bring together
to create spaces
to give up
the space
              in order to be free
to destroy in order to have space

to destroy in order to progress
to destroy in order to have been there

to destroy in order to destroy
to destroy in order to live

Schach mit Marcel Duchamp

ILSE TIELSCH

Ilse Tielsch (1929–   ) began writing in a traditional mode of nature poetry and developed a more critical stance. Social and cultural themes also find expression in her short stories and novels, for which she is well known. Selections here are from *Regenzeit* (1975) and *Nicht beweisbar* (1981); both at München: Delp.

What Belongs to Me

This table
this chair
this springtime
this sharply-whetted knife
this dead fish on the plate
this bread
this heartbeat
this moment of love
this thought
that does not betray me
this bird-call
this third cock-crow
this evening
this angst

and the cobweb
this thin
thread
hope

Regenzeit

We're Satisfied

The streets are good
we get there faster
than ever before
we are forgotten faster

The distances are getting smaller
the goals shrink
the ability to remember
decreases

The windows are sealed
the door locks are patented
we eat the soup lukewarm
we don't want
to burn ourselves

The murderers are still
on the way
we feel free of guilt
we don't take it so seriously

Thus dying
becomes easier

Nicht beweisbar

Not Provable

The house
in which I live
the table
at which I sit
the plate
from which I eat

the earth
on which I walk
with the insane
suspicion
that everything is real:

The house
the plate
the table

and I

Nicht beweisbar

Vita with Postscript

Born
given a name
remained strange
lost

the shadow there
on the way
that could be me

perhaps

Nicht beweisbar

The Walls of My House

Through the walls
of my house
come people
I didn't invite

Others
who are always
welcome
for whom I am still
waiting
never come

Nicht beweisbar

Final reply
to a first conversation
above brickyards
where the ground was
gorged
things written
and thought

No! moles
are no longer blind
they look inward

the grass is eternal
and dreams are realized
sometimes

The sign
the nocturnal street
the place where you
will always be

So that remembering
not be a form of forgetting
I light a candle
in Salzburg

(for Günter Eich)

Regenzeit

ANDREAS OKOPENKO

Andreas Okopenko (1930–   ) was born in Czechoslovakia and moved with his family to Vienna in 1939. A chemist by training, he works in industry. As a writer of social satire and political parody, he previously published three volumes of poetry that were recently collected in *Gesammelte Lyrik* (Wien: Jugend und Volk, 1980).

First Sunshine

You see, now you can squint a bit;
no, not so much, only enough so your eyelids are cool
    to your eyes.

You will still see the sky so blue
that you almost understand where the snow went so suddenly.
You wouldn't want to walk yet under the three poplars
    standing immediately over there.
But the crows are gone, and this morning I heard a real
    songbird.

Don't stay out too long at first;
but maybe tomorrow you can squint a bit more.
The sun will of course get brighter each day.
If nothing interferes, we'll soon have spring.

Gesammelte Lyrik

Summer Fragments

I. End of a Summer Sunday

The later afternoons
here are such
that one notices the slanting blue field-flowers
the later afternoons
here are sunny
the later afternoons
here go a long way

go across the street in its luster
over the fenced-in pastures
for cattle
go past
the defoliated green
hotel
go past
yet much more
and finally past—into the river.

Where to go with the pathos of your words?
Into the river bed, where green fields
are carved as with a cake-cutter
to give the brown water a path?
An address to the frogs? Hold a puddle lecture?
What else are your speeches? All of them.

Let's try once putting life on the scale.
Stop the surrogates. No paper.

Summer rainstorm eight in the evening
in the green sky
black contour

In the gray dawn around three, powerfully
(a rain-shower shortly before had washed the red-
drenched dreams from the face of the night)
the river bank all around is awakened

II. July Morning

Over the street, like a towel in the swimming pool,
lies the sunshine.
The windows play on the south side,
and all around
no one is out on the street.

Many blocks down a car is grazing,
the motor got out and is talking to a young dog
that lies on his white feet in the dust
or jumps around a bit in the morning.

———

In the woods I found
a love poem, spoken into a gas mask.

———

From a red root
I whittled small pencils.

———

From the trust that has come to an end
from the trust that should come to an end
the songs clatter my ears full.
But the pond, only now in April awakened, wanting now
to be eye-to-eye and never to come to an end
refreshes me anew infinitely.

———

In July the park holds summer in itself
holds in itself a single bird
that never stops singing

———

III. Brooding Afternoon in July

After the noon hour the sky is silent on the asphalt.
The trees are greenly silent. The paths in the park
are loose, long, and old . . .

Gesammelte Lyrik

Prose behind the Insanity

Please excuse me, Madam, if I constantly cough in your
    face.
It's against the rules, as I well know, of good etiquette.
But what does that mean today, when even the Geneva
    Conference can't be relied on to protect us fully.
You must excuse me, Madam, if I constantly cough in your
    face.
But since the last bacterial war my lungs are, as one
    says, somewhat affected.

Perhaps too, they were weakened by the cement dust that
    morning when I dug out a piece of coal with my
    fingers from under the house.
I didn't need the coal for heating (it was a warm early-
    September day) but that piece of coal was my wife.
Don't take it as a slight, Madam, if I here again
    emphasize: my wife was beautiful . . . and so young.
As one knows, sometimes it happens that a photograph
    bears more similarity to the original object than
    its own (altered) substance. Thus, for example,
    I never kiss the coal but only the paper.

You're going to the theater tonight?
Aren't you also, Madam, of the opinion that Jean-Paul
    Sartre bears some of the blame for the last war?
    You would like to talk with me about it? Tonight
    when you are alone, you say?
Madam, I deeply regret that other engagements prevent
    me from taking advantage of this generous offer.
    I have a very tight schedule, which it is not in
    my power to change; tonight, for example, I spit
    out my lungs.

No, I was not at the last garden party. Three orchestras,
    you say?
Between us, Madam: Are you convinced of the necessity
    of a fourth world war?

Gesammelte Lyrik

Edith

Since that afternoon when her girlfriend
sat in the backyard with Charlie,
Edith (even at school) thinks:

Strange—what is love anyway?
It's supposed, as the poets write,
to unite souls for eternity,
or something like that,
the poets write.

It's supposed, as her parents say,
to be the noblest of bonds,
the most refined of social conventions,
or, as her girlfriend says,
the most heroic of conquests.

But I have seen
only one thing, says Edith:
You must look like the cover-girl of a magazine,
or, better yet, like a chorus-girl in a club
where young people are not allowed.
Otherwise you don't get to have
the union of souls and such things.

Thus love must be
a show (youth not admitted)
or a magazine (in a brown wrapper).
Actually, though, you want it most
when you're young and not yet photographed,
thinks Edith.

She gets a bad grade
in that class
because she has immature thoughts
instead of those
in the lesson plan.
Besides, her teacher is shocked.

There remains for the human race,
thus endangered by her,
only one hope:

that even Edith will learn
not to question;
but refer instead
to the mirror in her purse
or a man.
That brings contentment,

and contentment is indispensable
for progress.
Otherwise it could happen
that some of us
might become human.

Gesammelte Lyrik

Bachelors and Language

1
Hannelore will thus be my wife.
Or: Hannelore thus will be my wife.
Such decisions would from then on be the most important ones.

2
The "Mary Ann" sank on May 19th,
and the captain was satisfied
that it was not with the "Hans Jörg" he went down.

3
I am completely transformed,
for I saw LINDA yesterday,
and how I long to meet LINDA tomorrow.

4
Hannelore will of course never be my wife.
I will of course never be a captain.
I will of course never meet Linda.

5
I'm sorry about the latter.
"Latter" is impermissible.
"I" with "sorry" is inadmissible.

Gesammelte Lyrik

GERHARD RÜHM

Gerhard Rühm (1930–   ) was co-founder and spokesman for the Vienna Group in the 1950s and 1960s, and he thus did much to initiate the movement of "experimental poetry." He is also a musician and composer of serial music. His poetry, which employs both visual and acoustic elements, is collected in *Gesammelte Gedichte und Visuelle Texte* (Reinbek: Rowohlt, 1970).

some things

on the table
is a gray cloth
on it an open pack of cigarettes
    shiny yellow and torn blue
next to that half a bottle of cherry rum
    (austrian label)
in front of it a typewriter with my fingers
to the left a ball-point pen
a notebook (orange-colored)
underneath it a piece of white paper with a poem
    title: february
next to that (near the edge of the table) an old folder
    it's closed (but I know what's in it)
and when I'm not typing my right arm is
    on the corner of the table
my face still hangs over it
it's twelve noon
the appearance of the table will soon change

e.g. becoming
our faces opposite each other
our mouths opening and closing
our hands with forks and knives in motion
our eyes meeting now and then

thus I ventured some predictions for the next
        quarter hour
and close
with a look
at the door

Gesammelte Gedichte

property is theft

my hair
my head
my eyes
my ears
my nose
my mouth
my neck
my arms
my hands
my torso
my balls
my penis
my woman
my vagina
my thigh
my knee
my calf
my feet
my shoes
my world
my brain

Gesammelte Gedichte

far
farther
and further furthering furthered
unlimited limitless
v o i d
and and and
spacelessly extended into free space
boundlessly unbounded in the free space and
endlessly wide in width widen wider
infinitely expanded in the far farther further furthermore
unununfathomable immeasurable beyond suddenly from afar
nearer
near
here
YOU

Gesammelte Gedichte

ALFRED KOLLERITSCH

Alfred Kolleritsch (1931–   ) is a prominent figure on the current literary scene, as a founding member of the "Forum Stadtpark" and editor of the journal *manuskripte*. His innovative role is documented in *Wie die Grazer auszogen, die Literatur zu erobern* (München: edition text & kritik, 1975), and his colleagues devoted a special issue of *manuskripte* (1981) to his honor. Selections are from his award-winning *Einübung in das Vermeidbare* (Salzburg: Residenz, 1978).

I don't trust my impressions.
Previously one just sat there
with a caved-in chest,
it began to bark: a hot anger,
a melancholy
with large prominent ears.

Now
I'm looking for traces,
trampled-down foliage,
a person who makes mistakes,
who annoys me,
who, when I come,
is gluing together a broken can cover
and doesn't look up.

Of course
I don't get used to it,
I notice
I have no habits.

The inside from earlier was borrowed,
outside, things are dispersed,
somebody pours out poetry,
a foregone opportunity.

I say to myself:
the heavy eyelids were preferable,
the finding more exciting
than the searching,
the found fodder
more enjoyable than the hunger.

Einübung in das Vermeidbare

It is increasingly less difficult to get up.
That's not a sign of happiness.
I go out of the house and see the burnt grass,
there is no dew on the benches and garden chairs,
the green garden hose
is not the garden hose
I dreamt of.

Then it occurs to me
that I forgot not to think of you.
Your presence seethes within me
with the old hum.
The peril of Zeno's tortoise remains
hard on my heels.
You go away, I stand still,
the distance changes nothing on the nearness.

Only the things I see
occur to me about myself,
every edge, every line is a border,
a bank where it stops.

Tables, bottles, gooseberry bushes,
a dried-up mouse,
I proffer myself
but not like a suction cup.
The utmost is the indifference
and its encyclopedia,
a summer morning with little joy
in reading farther in Flaubert's "Bouvard et Pécuchet."

From you there is no letter, no card.
I compare that
with what you said.
I am left over, so short
that I am indemonstrable,
violently vanished
quickly on the threshold.

Einübung in das Vermeidbare

This time we have not returned from a trip,
nor were we here,
we probably sat in rooms,
subject to the arbitrariness
of books, records, and letters,
silent,
sprinkled with radio programs,
trick films,
phone calls,
someone asked me:
"What do you think of language?"

We who abandon the way,
who search for more describable ways,
who wrap the remaining days
in calendars:
for later meaningless proofs
and reproaches,
for suspension bridges
above stagnating streams.

The two of us
with trap tendrils into strange things,
mocked by ourselves
as loners,
who in the days thereafter
work,
sketch,
choke on sentences,
soundless in the scream
that smothers the voice
of our history.

Einübung in das Vermeidbare

Thus pressed to the edge,
everything is inflexible for the flight.

I am proud
to be incapable
of taking the hurt as an excuse
to speak of healing.
Thus the hours define themselves,
then I say,
it was again a year.

A fall bouquet stands on the table,
red berries, grasses.
When I blow into it
or say your name out loud,
the thistle turns around.

In Ludwig Hohl's room
long after midnight
I hear the sentence,
"a wonderful expression:
I am at home."
It is the minus sign before death,
danced in from the small figure
under the strings and cards,
this faithfulness of the strings.

You are at home,
the uncertainty against the uncertainty
cancels it out,
but how good
we once knew it to be.

Einübung in das Vermeidbare

When a person writes
the doors don't close,
one question sticks to another,
one apprehension
reverses the next.

Thus the harmony breaks in
like ice that grows through steel,
and one feels the warm rippling
all around.

Then the eyes smart,
then one breaks the dearest thing,
then goodness is a strangle hold,
then one writes into emptiness
or says:
"Only up to the edge of a heart."

One says it to you,
before whom one has only a hand
to conceal oneself.

Einübung in das Vermeidbare

It wants to reveal itself as progress
at night
when one occasionally catches up with oneself,
the thoughts know the stream
that shares with other streams finally
only the name,
however deeply one may penetrate.

We remember only that
which leaves behind images,
we drive experiences
together into chains
and exhaustedly acknowledge
how unified we are.

Set down on the sandbanks,
we dream of stones.

Einübung in das Vermeidbare

The house is closed.
The doors and windows are deaf.
The flowers on the walls
get higher every day.
Soon the house will be overgrown
with a bouquet of blossoms.
Their fragrance will be strong,
the colors denser than silence.

The house thereby bids one
forget it. It goes out of mind,
the empty space fills itself
with names. They are tied up,
poured over with knots,
inseparable, forever.
What the flowers are called is unknown.

The parting brought the unapproachability
of fresh growth, of a frightened
untouchable springtime which locked out
the old inhabitants. They go in a circle,
they protect their eyes.
The trampled path gets deeper,
the earth wall grows tenaciously.

That is the bold power to take leave,
the power of the beautiful, the power to conceal.
Behind one's back the snow
fills up the footsteps. The sky trickles down,
the hot light that had come
through the window and the wind above the door
suffocate far under the flowers.

Einübung in das Vermeidbare

The night in which one re-reads the sentences
which forced one
to remain in the room
in the closet
shows:
the sentences,
they are frozen in the middle of the dance.

They lodge in memory,

they had touched their goal
with high speed
and moved, doubly quickened,
back to their place,
to the thousand other sentences.

At one time they warded off the pleasance,
the rose-thoughts.

They did not quiet the blood,
without regard for the middle level

in which all are pure
but don't live.

Nevertheless,
something warm, almost hot,
emerges,
the love, moreover,
that one said it so.

Einübung in das Vermeidbare

"These poems were anticipations
of actions," a friend wrote me.
They return through murky water,
hung with obstacles
on their way.
Now one could write
about the motives,
about the anger,
now, since it's time
to remember
in clear sentences
through tougher deeds.

What has been until now
has destroyed the trust,
sandbags grew in the joints,
behind me I heard
the angry cheerfulness calling.

The sun crackles and counsels
to carry things away.

It means to observe moderation
in the flights of fancy.
A new longing,
which spreads itself broad,
promises worse things.

One becomes powerless,
powerless against the dreams,

on the way to recovery
an illness entices,
it is the will of the illness.

Thus the impatience receives
the other name,
it is called patience;
it is the patience
through it all to call everything by its name.

The poems, the curls and small rolls,
the cork lines in each crack
become soft.

A desire for natural signs
tramples the metaphor into the earth,

it is the hope
of seeing things differently:
the world as a joint effort
in which feelings are disseminated,
also the observation
that it continues.

Einübung in das Vermeidbare

KONRAD BAYER

Konrad Bayer (1932–64) was prominent as jazz musician, director of an art gallery, and a leading figure among the Viennese *bohème*. He joined h. c. artmann and others in 1958 to form the Vienna Group, which produced literary cabaret, experimental films, avantgarde magazines, and "happenings." After his suicide at the age of thirty-six, his literary work was edited and published by his fellow-poet Gerhard Rühm as *der sechste sinn* (1966) and later as *Das Gesamtwerk* (1977), both at Reinbek: Rowohlt.

for judith

when monday drives the roses through the ground
i stand at the window and wait

when tuesday dashes the rain on the shore
then i stand at the window and dance

when wednesday for wednesday divides the sun
i stand at the window and cry

when thursday loses its cross in the park
i leave the window with approaching step

when friday beats its clothes into the clouds
then i stand at the window and betray you twice

when saturday finds its hair in the chimney
then i stand at the window and sing

when sunday gives death away gratis
then i stand at the window and wait

Das Gesamtwerk

we won't pay any attention to this invitation
we'll put it in the file
we'll bury it
we'll burn it
we'll cut it up with the new scissors
we'll turn it around
we'll give it away
we'll lose it
we'll exchange it
we'll forget it
but we know what we owe to this invitation

Das Gesamtwerk

franz war.   franz was.
war franz?   was franz?
franz.   franz.
war.   was.
wahr.   true.
war wahr.   was true.
wirr.   confused.
wir.   we.
franz, wir!   franz, we!
wir, franz.   we, franz.
ihr.   you.
franz war wirr.   franz was confused.
war franz irr?   was franz mistaken?
wirrwarr.   confusion.

Das Gesamtwerk

[Translator's note: A translation of the poem is provided for the semantic content, but the reader is encouraged to read the poem aloud in German, since the effect of the poem depends upon the phonetic similarity of its sounds.]

ERNST DAVID

Ernst David (1932–   ) lives in his native city of Vienna, where he works for the government. His poetry has been translated into Serbo-Croatian and other languages of southeastern Europe. The present English translations are drawn from his volume *Erfahrungen* (Baden: Grasl, 1976), as well as from the journal *Podium* (1980).

six haiku

prevailing west wind
the cloud over the mountain
seems to stand still

solitary crow
upward over the summit
rising in the wind

as if the first time
seeing trees glowing gold-brown
glowing red in rock

walking home at night
after long hours of work
empty fully leached

off the beaten track
how absolute the stillness
unlimited snow

strewn out in the smog
the handful of haiku drifts
downward toward the street

Podium

under the trapeze

if the air is absent
the salto mortale
takes place in a liquid medium

the performer's hands are
painted with signs of victory
free of all care
he laughs silently

incredible laugh

the spectator's consciousness
is altered
decisively

Erfahrungen

listen to the voice at its root
in its kernel
listen to its beginning

you meet an obstacle
overcome it

suddenly
you are surrounded by a net of vibrations
listen to the inaudible frequencies
let ultra- and infra-sound ring in you

don't remain there
go farther

to the source
of all audibility   all visibility

there a large stillness
a vacuum you say

you're right
a great stillness

let it enter you
        occupy you
penetrate it

an initial impulse
a first beginning
will then come to you

Erfahrungen

after going astray in the underbrush

having found the WAY
beginning to take it
learning to grasp it
gradually
with my feet

seeing clouds trees
touching the grass with my fingers
joining in with life

baggage left behind

heightening awareness
gaining confidence
to discard disappointments

becoming simpler
like the WAY

Erfahrungen

ELFRIEDE GERSTL

Elfriede Gerstl (1932–   ) lives as a free-lance writer in Vienna and also occasionally in Berlin. She is associated with the Graz Authors, and her writing is highly experimental, displaying a mixture of coquetry and irony with ambivalence and charm. Selections are from *spielräume* (Linz: edition neue texte, 1977). Her most recent volume, *wiener mischung* (1982, at the same experimental publishing house in Linz), unfortunately appeared too late for inclusion here.

Höbinger

1: Bremer
2: Emerson
3: Grit
4: Linda
5: Nebhut
6: Rettenbacher
7: Georg Bendl

1   Höbinger has been lying in bed now for three days
2   without being sick
4   without being physically ill
5   he just doesn't feel like doing anything
6   he doesn't sufficiently feel like doing anything
3   he doesn't sufficiently feel like it
4   maybe he's only in love

7   that passes
5   didn't he want to become a psychiatrist at one time
7   that passes
1   he looks pale
3   he looks better
4   he has red spots in his face
5   he wants to understand so many things
2   he wants to change so many things
1   he wants so much to understand and change (himself)
6,7   that passes
      that passes
1,2,4 we want to visit him
  4,5 let's visit him
3,6,7 we visited him
5   the thought that the world is different from what he would like
      doesn't cross his mind
3   he's in his mind
7   is that a reason to despair
4   I don't know
6   well when one (like) he is
1   he doesn't know that he doesn't change anything
2   he doesn't know that everything goes on
4   that everything goes on as if it were temporary
6   that we for example are going to the movies one door down
      without him
7   what doesn't all simply go on
3   what all doesn't simply go on
5   death
      death doesn't simply go on
4   stop
5   death is a straight matter
      death doesn't pass
      death isn't temporary
2   stop
6   we don't get any farther that way
7   we wanted to go to the movies
1,7   we wanted for sure to go to the movies
6   that way we don't get any farther

spielräume

Cornbush, the name Cornbush
Cornbush spreads his arms out as if he wanted to bless

the waiting herd of cars, he's a traffic cop on his
work days, or
Cornbush is a gas man in the suburbs, dog owner,
beer consumer, despiser of women, or
Cornbush, the north-suburbs stove man with a secret vice
Cornbush, the trouser dealer with the smell of rose water
and onion skin
the old Cornbush
the young Cornbush
Cornbush who for years hasn't touched anything
Cornbush who for years hasn't been touched by anything
Cornbush in rivalry with Cornbush
Cornbush is not yet lost
the old Cornbush with a wooden leg and matches
Cornbush in coming
Cornbush makes people
Cornbush Cornbush above all
from child to Cornbush
Hello Cornbush
Cornbush I want to be called
Cornbush I would want to be called if Cornbush hadn't gone
    around
with buttons in 1923
Cornbush I want to be called when he's no more
the Cornbush
Cornbush is a tree
Cornbush is a tree in the desert and in the grain mill
when Cornbush meets Cornbush in the street in
the desert and says
Hello Cornbush

spielräume

HERMANN JANDL

Hermann Jandl (1932–   ) is a published poet in his own right, although he stands in the shadow of his brother Ernst Jandl. The present selections appeared in the journal *Podium* (1975, 1980, 1982) and in the anthology *Zeit und Ewigkeit* (Düsseldorf: claassen verlag, 1978).

successful attempt

I tried
to live like others
with wife and children
a plot of land

and red roses
I didn't achieve
any of that
therein I see a
successful attempt

Podium

happiness

but for a hair's breadth
I would have died last night

luckily
I still have it

bad mirror

a glance in the mirror reveals
it bears no resemblance to me

the jogger from schönbrunn

I run
I run because
I run

I see the beautiful flowers
just like the king does
he has the same kind of eyes

I have two legs
a left one and a right one
I run with both legs

today is ideal sailing weather
the queen can undoubtedly sail
as little as I

I run fast
I run intensely
above all I like to run

I run by the yellow house
just like the president
runs by the white one

now I'm running in place
I bring my knee to my chin
I live because I run

the reading

let your beard grow
schedule a poetry reading
black suit (perhaps Rent-Al)
a serious look

dignified
set
clock on table
read very slowly

pause ten seconds after each line
better yet fifteen seconds
speak softly
mistakes add to the effect of the evening

enter the auditorium
ten people are a large audience
smile   nod
perhaps a hand-gesture

sit
light lucky strike with candle
inhale   look at audience

smile
take a deep breath
look at the audience again
read

Zeit und Ewigkeit

it

it's coming
you feel it
it's coming
you have no defense

you walk faster
remain standing
run your hands through your hair
rub your eyes

take a deep breath
close your eyes tightly
lie down

get up again

you feel
and know
it's
coming

it comes again and again
enters without asking
settles in firmly
sticks to things sticks

bores bores itself in
yells falls silent
kneads presses hops circles
burns bites pulls sucks

it's there
you don't give up
you don't want to give up
you must not give up

you turn on the light
you turn off the light
rush into the bathroom
from there to the kitchen

back to the other room
from there to another
back to the first one
back and forth

you get a hold of yourself
you don't ask
you don't think
your thoughts run wild

you swallow unclear words
you throw up
but you still know
who you are

which key fits the top lock
which the bottom
where the cigarettes are
where the alcohol is

how to get into bed
but the president died
but the milk is sour
but the military marches on

Podium

OTTO LAABER

Otto Laaber (1934–73) studied psychology and English literature, spending a year as an exchange student in Lafayette, Indiana. He later withdrew from public life and, like Bayer, Fritsch, and Kräftner, committed suicide while still relatively young. His poetry gives evidence of a sensitive, intense nature, with premonitions of futility. His work was posthumously published as *Inventur* (Baden: Grasl, 1976).

Inventory

There remain
imprinted
comparable illusions
similar farewells

occasional disappointments
some indifference
every attempted relation
every renunciation
interchangeable

Many long summer evenings
rivers and landscapes
the beginning of a friendship
fog cloud-cocoons
the attempted conversation
the sum of lonely evenings
—yours and mine—
the product of all empty fall days

every sobering thought every loss
the caution—the joy—deliberately
cultivated illusions
the statistics of life

For personal memories
much effort
hardly communicable
imprinted
for ourselves
you and me
weighed out

something comparable:
the statistical result

Inventur

Collected Time

We collect time
time that belongs to no one
dust-gray time of the streets
asphalt-time of the nights in cities
We save time as a possession
I collect it for you
you save it for me
we wait
the opportunity for discussion
not even the attempt will take place
we keep time ready
we know what will come: nothing
we must only wait
be ready for no one, nothing
the gray land grows by itself
the contingent will not occur

Inventur

These Days

Our city has sunk to the bottom of the sea
with all its streets, all its buildings.
Schools of fish swim through the open windows,
solitary crab occupy the TV station.

The news media have been converted;
a wave sweeps, not your hair, but algae along.
Many people go for a walk at the bottom of the sea
or go about their business, briefcase in hand.

The big sea-monsters loiter in the basements
and darken the water with violet ink.
These days it has sunk to the bottom of the sea,
our city, without warning, with all its buildings.

Inventur

Positive

In agreement
(between two suicide attempts)
with the habits of the winds—
long accustomed
to the aspirations of the grasshopper—
become tolerant
of temperature fluctuations in April
positively disposed
(between two suicide attempts
with inadequate means)
toward autumn days, cloud-fields, and
similar diffuse configurations
myself a participant
(secret accomplice)
in the diversions of the winds

Inventur

September Heath

Listening to
the earth's code
on the September heath
Wanting to decipher
the messages of summer
in the remaining twilight
Like any day
unclarified
in the branches of birch trees
the last signals of sun

Inventur

Who says

Who says that death
will be dark?
A grave for desire?
A sack over one's head?
Perhaps he will come
with bells and trumpets,
a jester in fool's clothing,
a rogue, a rascal,
who fetches you
for a country festival!

Inventur

From the Milky Way

No farther
than to the Milky Way
wander the cloud lambs.
Milk-drinking makes
immortal being more bearable.

On the other side
black winds blow,
holes gape,

the world a bellows
stretched with
endless skin.

Inventur

GERALD BISINGER

Gerald Bisinger (1936–   ) lives as a free-lance writer in both Berlin and Vienna, where he is a noted critic and editor of h. c. artmann's work. Illustrative of his experimental stance is the cycle represented below, which is intended to be read aloud, from *7 Gedichte zum Vorlesen* (Berlin: Literarisches Colloquium, 1968). The repetitive circlings also illustrate the "search for identity" in the tension between the two diverse locations, as well as the different levels of past time as (non-)related to the present.

At Lake Lietzen
or
The Search for Identity

An evening like that at the bookshelf that is at times
no idyll is rather a search for identity
a digging a grubbing a leafing through to recover
the past who was I who am I who am
I thus years years and days (it's that way in
Gustafsson) I trace the past I
am amazed at that time what did I read then w-
rite and about what why and where that
year and before and later what writ-
ten read why then in Vienna in Berlin be-
ginning of '64 in this room in that year read
wrote at the desk here Witzleben Street
16 Charlottenburg right in the area of the po-

lice station or from Lake Lietzen as you wish '64
and today what am I writing here what have I read

I read I reacted I wrote lit-
erature produced literature out of myself through
my I what is that the red sandstone bridge over
Lake Lietzen the dirty barred-off area under-
neath one doesn't get through there in a boat the new
Kant Street above it the noise of traffic of ro-
tating wheels the short stretch the red sandstone
bridge it doesn't thrill you it has this short
stretch a main thoroughfare I leaf through an
issue of a literary magazine from October '61 then the
wall was new in Berlin topical Döblin
Georg Heym and this poem from van Hoddis "At
Lake Lietzen" when was it written why dedicated
to Georg Heym he's in it had drowned already in
nineteen hundred twelve (in another lake)

The red sandstone bridge from that time and today
I touch it what does identity mean I I
live right near Lake Lietzen and I
went for a walk a year ago with this or that day
added or subtracted at Lake Lietzen with Sophie
years years and days Gustafsson calls it
and then farther on in the line like one egg with
another identity in sixty-six walk at
Lake Lietzen fog-screened air with Sophie in
early fall at Lake Lietzen weeping willow is the
name of the tree with thin pliant branches
hanging down in the water waterbirds at
Lake Lietzen various species of duck in summer they
don't shy away from the boats simply withdraw on the
lake in the summer to sun themselves in a boat

Another summer a year and a day I rent
a boat row out a bit to sun myself
alone in the boat on the lake I see the TV
tower closer on the other side the new hotel it's
called Lakeview one can read it now I knew when
was it still a building site what was there years ago
a fall in '61 I was in Vienna and van Hoddis
long dead Sophie where was she where is she now
years years and days the red sandstone bridge
thrills you wrote van Hoddis one doesn't write that way
any more it has a main thoroughfare I see
that the wall six years old already is repaired
modernized in places removed is the Roman

barbed wire what was there before I didn't know it
then I didn't know Lake Lietzen did not not know Sophie

An evening like that at the bookshelf this digging the
grubbing the leafing through and associating who was I
who am I who am I therefore this search for
identity to find perchance the past a single issue
of the magazine like that a poem like "At Lake Lietzen"
years years and days the red sandstone bridge over
the dirty area Lake Lietzen to the right and Lake Lietzen
to the left but still not like one egg with another identi-
ty what is that Berlin Georg Heym and Jakob van
Hoddis at Lake Lietzen '61 the wall years years ago
and years with Adolf Hitler days I sit at m-
y desk here Witzleben Street 16 Charlotten-
burg today and now right in the area of the po-
lice station or from Lake Lietzen as you wish identi-
ty the red sandstone bridge tomorrow I'll touch it

7 Gedichte zum Vorlesen

JUTTA SCHUTTING

Jutta Schutting (1937–   ), as author of both prose and poetry, is a highly conscious and reflective writer who is prominent on the current literary scene. She holds a Ph.D. in literature and history but gave up a teaching career to devote full time to writing. Selections are from *In der Sprache der Inseln* (1973), which was followed by *Lichtungen* (1976), both at Salzburg: O. Müller, and her recent volume, *Liebesgedichte* (Salzburg: Residenz, 1982).

Doves

I fed this dove
when the word dove had become something without reference
    to real doves
and this one when the word in a poem
was a synonym for message
and this one when in a love poem
a dove in the last line was something different from the dove
    in the first line
and this one
when a dove, a twig in its beak,
was no longer a sign that emerged from an image
but a dove again, a twig in its beak

and this one
when the word in a poem
was for me an evasion and idle enchantment

In der Sprache der Inseln

Trees

I planted this tree
when I saw a tree for the first time
and this one when the word spoken in front of a tree
became its name
and this one when I first saw the word written
and this one and this one
when the word tree first called forth
an image of tree and I thus comprehended
that the word represents the object it names
and this one when standing in front of a bush I understood
   what a tree was
and this one when the image tree became
the outline of an evergreen tree
and this one when I was surprised
that there are only specific trees
and this one when I assumed
that tree exists as such
and this one when tree was above all
the German word for arbor

And this one I dug up
when I discovered
that although the sound may evoke the concept
it is not thereby determined

In der Sprache der Inseln

Poems

a poem is something in the midst of a white plane
fenced in by itself and enclosed by the surface of its lines.
although it has forgotten where and how it came to be,
it is no lost soul
(for in that it reflects only itself, it also reflects
the situation from which it arose).
a poem is a window opened to a strange reality
behind which only the reality of the poem is visible
or a wall with blind windows
the ephemeral butterfly before it returns to dust
an injured seal
a sign—and image-script of mutually contradictory images and
   signs

a conch without the sound of the ocean
the bewitching hour of an object
an apple on a winter tree but not a rose frozen by hoar-frost
something that reminds one of something of which there is no
    memory
the last in a series of images diminishing into infinity
a sign of something for which there are signs only in poems
the reconstruction of something not even dreamed
something that speaks with itself in subterranean springs, plays
    shunting yard,
strings phases of the moon on a chain and invests words with
    landscapes
an island of speech, a reflection in a blind mirror
something that joins words with images that come into being
    only through this action
a forged bank check
a constellation that does not correspond to its name
a house door in the middle of a meadow, a piece of carpet in
    a burned-down house
a football game as a pretext for players to stage encounters
    with colors and lines
the difference between a real and a painted dove
a pure presence
each poem is a shell around a kernel possibly invented
each poem is a translation of the one poem that exists only in
    translation
each poem is its own condition
a poem is that which declares itself to be a poem

In der Sprache der Inseln

Interpretations

every poem is addressed to itself.
a poem is made
(but more discovered then invented).
angel in the first line means something different
from angel in the last line.
the essence of a poem is its meaning.
the meaning of a single noun
is determined by its importance within the line
and the difference from other nouns
in that their everyday meaning
is brought into a hypothetical relationship

with an as yet undefined word.
the existing nouns have a common denominator
to be discovered through the leading words.
adjectives are a border correction.
the verb *to be* is the main word in a poem:
it determines its state in partial equations.
every other verb only establishes relations—
the accusative object, directly connected to the subject,
comes in its wake,
through a prepositional object resistance is created
to the dominance of the subject,
between subject and dative of interest
the accusative object forms a neutral zone.
the effect of a poem
results from the contest of priorities
between given and private associations.
a boat that approaches
is different from a boat that one boards.

In der Sprache der Inseln

Clouds

Clouds that are barely still clouds
and those that play with the resemblance cloud—island,
    cloud—bush, or cloud—fire
and those that reflect the consciousness of being a cloud
and those that are images of themselves
and those that vary a possibility of their cloud-being
and those that as pure conception are only a pause in the sky
and those that, long since dissolved, later find a sky in
    themselves

In der Sprache der Inseln

a dove-late afternoon

a dove-late afternoon
drowsy light of the November wings
in its beak a message of the first snow

the smile hidden in its plumage
the light goes back into itself
all signs become suspended
we dive deeply into the twilight
what occurs is an image in a mirror

In der Sprache der Inseln

you can

you can
restore melted snow
call birds back
transform geometric figures into star images
divide everyday objects into sacred chapters
still the thirst of a lion
make the unicorn place a tangent on the moon
build graduated landscapes from words
change a flour sack into an air balloon
reassign the weights of scales

you can renew the dried-up well

In der Sprache der Inseln

I dedicate to you

all unwritten poems
all mediating thoughts
all oceans and islands
all moon all ironbed
all smells that go directly to the heart
all that relates to you, thus everything
all that does not already belong to you, thus nothing
all unread books, all postponed work
all undeciphered scripts that long before were addressed to you
all cessation of time, all inbetween times
all illegality all prayers all risks
all blues all greens
all words that through you have a new meaning
all conversations as veiled allusions, thus all

all poplar and heliotrope
all fear all joy of deception
all images of ladies with lions
all children's toys all lye-steeped being
all hand-bells and hot-air balloons
all that blends well like non-colorfast clothes
a sailboat and a sea
a glass of water and a requiem for a rose

and above all the sea as I loved it before seeing it

In der Sprache der Inseln

Kinsey Report

Dream- or angel-honey
dream tears or dream drops
lighting with the aid of various techniques
maintained for hours:
rubbing oneself on angel smiles, gently brushing over evening
    prayers
sleeping naked with the dreams
extending the heavenly vision
soul kiss or deep-well kiss, simple lip-blossom kiss
speaking with angel tongues
hurried angel adventures in house doors, in cars, at parties
touch of angel wings and prayer fluff
meetings with guys or girls
who have already had visions
the most frequent position in angel conversations:
the soul on top, the body below
driving angel visitations to extreme exhaustion
no proof that the frequency of high-morning prayers
devalues the nightly calls
having contact with annunciatory angels
but also with professional guardian angels
many of these men meditate in the dark
in order to concentrate better on their systems of belief
many of these children learn something
that comes near to a real vision

the sudden release from the tension
when the angel with the lily steps out of its image

Liebesgedichte

Blundering

a house wall that I must climb down to get to you,
but already after a few groping steps toward you,
the nakedness begins to tremble, I start to slide.
an apartment building many floors high, the descent
blocked by suitcases, furniture, and propped-open doors,
thus I climb down, so as not to miss you,
the precarious
railing inclining with me toward you,
but before I get to your door,
I fall from the rust-red railing-blossom past you.
it's a rocky path I climb down,
but the more I, so as not to miss you again,
press down through the barbed wire constraining me,
the more I entangle myself
in its climbing roses and the fear,
with anticipated joy of each thorn in the flesh,
to have gone the wrong way.
a chimney climb,
that, since all gondolas are on strike,
should lead down from the glacier to you in Berlin,
but dizzy with impatience
and uneasy with fear of reunion,
I let myself, panting, be enclosed by the walls
instead of falling toward you in the valley—

so far, even in dream, is
the way from your cheek to your mouth.

Liebesgedichte

a first vacation day
our carefreeness suddenly overshadowed by despondency,
bearable only through the thought
that much of that which is simply to be born
will consolingly falsify itself
through the disconsolate-consolatory nearness of the other
(whose disconsolation at the nearness of the other
in reality makes all that so unbearably in need of consolation),
the more irretrievably these days, when they are over, are gone

the longed-for days are however still here,
it's only the first day of the cursed happiness—

the reluctance to break off the togetherness
that is not, even together, to be restored,
each touch of the hand throws us back farther into ourselves,
bearable only by virtue of the undamaged confidence
that memory will hold this day or these days
momentarily very differently in remembrance,
as if it were inconsolable disconsolation
over numbered days

but the longed-for days are still here,
it's only the first day of the unused happiness—
basement air that blows me
out of all the sisterly-brotherly shared observations,
chills of the soul, so near to you,
as hard to misunderstand as the impudence of the souvenir
    landscape,
and despondency as hard to misinterpret
as desolation at activities
which are innocent of the disturbance,
but for us not to be forgotten:

self-forgettingly devoted to our attempt at comfort and
    consolation,
you too forget that you are with me—
everywhere here where we are now for the first time
already has the echo of having been there together,
all the love that we say to ourselves is already clouded by sadness
with which we, each for himself or herself,
will let these discomforting-comforting words return

Liebesgedichte

Water Glass

high noon,
the only thing remaining in an empty glass,
makes the disconnectedness of everything
that has been
read like a card from heaven—
never again flowers on the rim of the water glass
that your lips won't touch again,
impotence of the ox that must bleed
one with the debility at the thought
that someone after you and like you will hold the glass.
water that mocks its source

and pain that belies its origin,
high noon, filled with the thirst of remembering—
the bread on the table
from which you broke off a piece,
is so much at one with the strangeness of everyday things
that the absence of your hand
hollows out my belief
and the emptiness of separation comes over the table

but then all unreconciliation is drunk away,
the return of distanced signs
fills itself up with our words

Liebesgedichte

HERMANN GAIL

Hermann Gail (1939–   ) grew up under difficult childhood conditions and received one of the most severe prison sentences ever administered to an adolescent. He has since been paroled and lives as a writer, characterizing the milieu he knows so well and protesting against the many forms of social injustice. Selections are from *Weiter Herrschaft der weissen Mäuse* (Baden: Grasl, 1979).

Sunday Morning in the Park

The park I'm describing
has no elegant garden layout
where English greyhounds promenade
and chic movie stars hang out
In my park children learn to smoke
and mothers warn their teen-age
sons against cheap women
In general the foreigners and the dogs
are a majority in this park
of course the foreigners stink
and the dogs stink
and the rats run around in the sand boxes
and the Yugoslavs build a
tower of dirt and urine
while the shiny pile of dog shit
is covered with flies . . .
But I am merely a black-white poet

the most important things for me are
black and white
above all black
tough and threatening
dead weight
and never a golden star in the sky
above all black
and no white
I implore you: Give me more white
destroy the dangerous weapons
spread a warm cloak over poverty
and blindness and blood-thirsty Dobermans
then I will gladly write about the
lilies in spotless snow
about the lilies of a young girl in
an ermine cape

Weiter Herrschaft der weissen Mäuse

Visit to the Juvenile Penitentiary

Gerasdorf, June 23, 1978

Before entering I drink a glass
of red wine in the cafe across the street
and look for the pissoir in the back yard
Then an iron gate swings open
like those at elegant villas
and a friendly guard greets me
the other rooms are blank-white
and everything here is blank-white and aseptic
and I sit at a blank-white table
and read the poems I brought
and I know I cannot win
the trust of these young men
with my stories

Most of the youth who do penance
here with their days and their years
look at me indifferently
they are perhaps sad, afraid and despondent
I notice immediately: my words don't mean much to them
and I read rather softly and haltingly
and think: maybe it would have been better

if I had brought a carton of Marlboro or Kent
or a poster with the curves of a Monroe
or a small bird
or a guinea pig

I am told that the director is competent
all doors are open during the day
at night there are no disturbing noises
and each one has a clean bed
and there is a library
and an athletic field and even a swimming pool
The modern reformatory fulfills almost
all dreams I say as I leave
and a guard who smells of perfume
softly closes the human cage
behind me

Weiter Herrschaft der weissen Mäuse

Description of an American Billionaire

The first event in his career is
quite ordinary and reveals neither his genius
nor his character: in his youth he
buys a cheap boat that had sunk
repairs it with great patience
and sells it again at large profit
Later he joins a shipping firm
and soon owns more ships than the
"Golden Greeks" Niarchos and Onassis together
His sphere of influence extends to the military
and of course also to private magnates

He walks to the office
he doesn't smoke
he avoids alcohol
his favorite beverage is buttermilk
he doesn't have a car
he doesn't have a plane
he lives very modestly
his name does not decorate a yacht
his meals are spartan
his billions are without heir

On the 35th floor of the company office
despite his 80 years
he still thinks of new projects

Weiter Herrschaft der weissen Mäuse

Explanation

A writer is a justice of the peace, a father confessor, a
police-officer.

(Max Jacob)

Whenever I read that poem
—Description of an American Billionaire—
at a poetry reading
someone in the audience
says reproachfully
that I am defending capitalism
that in spirit I probably even admire
IBM Texaco Ford GM
DuPont Standard Oil
Bayer Krupp Rockefeller
and conglomerates
my text doesn't indict
doesn't give the death blow
to the dying bourgeois

Yes
I am merely a poet
and I drink a glass of water
in the warm auditorium
and you entrenched behind
mountains of political books
you who beat the drums on your belly
and you who demand of me
that I be more than a poet—
I cannot be more
than radically against injustice
radically against falsity
radically against lack of freedom

Weiter Herrschaft der weissen Mäuse

LIESL UJVARY

Liesl Ujvary (1939–   ) was born in Pressburg, Czechoslovakia, and she holds a Ph.D. in Slavic literature from the University of Zurich. She also studied in Moscow and taught in Japan before moving to Vienna, where she lives as a free-lance writer. In her experimental texts from *sicher & gut* (Wien: Rhombus, 1977), language is consciously employed for trivial statements, intended paradoxically to break through the barriers of our conventional patterns of thought and speech.

Foreword to *sicher & gut*

This textbook is intended for all areas of life. It is a book for the inner as well as the outer "understanding." Language is here not only language in the narrow sense, language is here everything: fashion, ideology, material, furniture, architecture, means and purpose of life, etc.

Any standardized behavior can just as easily be seen as a language; as understandable for anyone, as equally useful for and usable by anyone; as a point of departure for possible criticism by anyone; as self-insight perhaps. This may appear amusing, terrible, ignorant, or whatever, depending upon interpretation: in any case no advice will be given here that would make the reader into a victim—the reader is here above all beneficiary.

As author I continually ask: why precisely this world which presents itself to us simply in the way that we initially grasp it. I mean thereby the dullness of a world of yes or no, of right angles, of the decimal system, that world of familiar orders.

288

Let's try to get away from these prefabricated images of the mind by insight into them, to break through the barriers of our cultural consciousness . . .

Everything has its Reason

From beer you get a beer-belly.
Whoever saves diligently can buy himself a nice kitchen.
Women have children.
When it rains the streets become empty.
Cars are practical. They pollute the air.
There's a military dictatorship now in Chile.
One plus one equals two.
In this country anyone can make something out of himself.
Whoever can't do anything can't make anything out of himself.
You reap what you sow.
The driver was lucky and suffered only mild injury.
Murder out of jealousy.
Yugoslavs meet at the south train station.
The research on UFOs in the United States is secret.
The military serves as defense for the country.
The traffic regulations.

sicher & gut

Important!

Rainer Pichler always says the same thing.
   "I have it all at my place."

Bodo Hell always says the same thing.
   "The phone rings constantly."

Uta Prantl always says the same thing.
   "Weekends we're not there."

Walter Ramstorfer always says the same thing.
   "Let's talk about that some other time."

Günter Leikauf always says the same thing.
   "I can't stay long."

Hannes Schneider always says the same thing.
   "That should be blown away."

Bernt Burchhart always says the same thing.
   "You have poetry in your blood."

Elfriede Gerstl always says the same thing.
   "I'm urgently looking for an apartment."

Gerwalt Brandl always says the same thing.
   "Tuesday evenings I can't."

Liesl Ujvary always says the same thing.
   "I still have to work."

sicher & gut

leave everything the way it is

the government governs
the street is dusty
austria is a neutral country
the forest is deforested
grammar is applied
workers are respectful to their overseers
the rule on escalators is: stand on the right walk on the left
the rights of citizens are limited
women love "triumph"
freedom is indivisible
some people promise each other eternal love
farmdale h-milk stays fresh three months
tomorrow is tuesday the 8th of october 1974
for dinner there's potatoes and blood sausage
the garden is full of weeds a foot high
the dishes are dirty
there are 2 towels and 1 shirt in the drawer

sicher & gut

HEIDI PATAKI

Heidi Pataki (1940–   ) writes satirical, provocative verse, uniting language experimentation with social criticism. The crisis of language is expressed in theoretical statements, as well as in later poems that remain largely untranslatable, since meaning is on nonsemantic levels. Selections are from *Schlagzeilen* (Frankfurt: Suhrkamp, 1968) and *stille post* (Linz: edition neue texte, 1978).

Eleven Theses about Poetry

1. *Poems must reflect current consciousness.*
A poem has no future, only a present.

2. *Lyric is a kind of fashion.*
We not only dress fashionably—we also talk so. The poem is a product of vogue.

3. *Individualism is antiquated.*
"Everything proceeds," says Lévi-Strauss, "as if each individual in our civilization had his/her own personality as a totem."
That is uneconomical. In these poems the individual no longer transforms its private feelings; rather, it reduces itself to catchwords.

4. *Originality is nonsense.*
Any sentence we might say has already been said a thousand times before. Thus the meaning has been lost: use destroys meaning.

5. *Épater la bohème!*
The confinement of ordered life produces its counterpart in the private desire for the anarchy of the artist.
What is this! Anarchical is only the order. Order as anarchy—that is the message of these poems.

6. *A poem must leave its reader disarmed.*
After experiencing a poem a reader won't dare to open his/her mouth.

7. *One can no longer write a new poem.*
Every poem quotes its predecessors. Thus these poems unscrupulously use for their purposes the entire history of literature: nothing, not even Goethe, remains sacred. Literary history becomes the waxworks of the muses.

8. *Language has become unusable.*
Each person is separated from all others by an assembly of prejudices. We suffer not from unintelligibility but from misunderstanding. These poems renounce any claim of establishing a kind of intelligibility. They take misunderstanding by its word: syntactic metaphors.

9. *The world breaks down into aggressions.*
Sadism is the most vital form of human communication. Only when we hurt the other person do we notice him/her. The rest is convention.

10. *A poem is not a lesson but rather an image of the world. Lyric is transcendental.*
Transcendental philosophy investigates the possibilities of all experience. But is experience even possible any more? In place of experience cliché has stepped in. Clichés are the material of the poem.

11. *Literature is a game of language.*
It differs in no way from car racing, chain smoking, cooking rice, or visiting a museum. Literature is a way of life. Not necessarily the most interesting way, but it passes the time.

Schlagzeilen

nature morte

who has you then you pretty wood?
and when? and why? how long? how soon?
a hoar-frost fell? "strawberry fields"?
one says? may be? and nice good night?
do you have words? never yet heard?

did you not promise? this and that?
o head of blood? and on the whole?
with open eyes? and pupils wide?
what for? how come? and black & white?
o christmas tree? in garden grown?
the pulse okay? where were you then?
there is a reaper what's his name?
diethylamid? what can that be?
for sure? sometimes? and never more?
the birds are silent in the wood?
behind the wood? what do I know?
and marijuana? all the more?

yesyes nono / who knows / perhaps
tomorrow when the rooster crows

Schlagzeilen

you have taken my language away

you have taken my language away

hungry i must run through the streets
in search of words of garbage
rummage through waste cans
for unsightly words thrown a-
way worn out

ask the newsboy if
there isn't a word missing on his coat
the milkman if there aren't words
for sale in bottles
the seagulls on the danube canal
if they don't carry words
on their wings from the black sea

the wind that comes from the east
and brings with it dust
why no words

how well a glowing grain of sand
a word from the sahara could grow here in the gravel
what a large crop i could harvest
on the kahlenberg in the fall

or the wind that comes from the west
a word from reims
what a pretty hedge i could prune
in the spring

a word from eisenstadt too
flown into my eye with the silt
what a pointed little knife i could
hammer out in the winter

but even the wind is still
and speaks of austria

you have taken my language away

Schlagzeilen

on the journey to your heart

if the doorkeeper denies
access to the collarbone
i'll force myself darkly
through the pupil of your eye

under the taut palate
i steer down your throat

feed on your adam's apple
for your breastbone is greedy
chops at me and would like to see
me nailed to your sacrum

quickly the veins open up
I wade through blue grottos
effervescing vaults of stalactitic caverns

through the foliage of your shoulder blades
i strike with the lobes of the lungs
do gymnastics in the branches of the bronchia
on the wide rib meadow

your breath comes whistling in

nearer and nearer i press
toward the thin purple chamber
bellows of your heart
rumbling it snaps open and shut

here i want to nest forever
poke bubbles in the glow
with my rod so it burns

here in front of your awful chamber
i want to spin a cocoon

become a chrysalis a maggot
that slowly eats away at your heart

Schlagzeilen

hosanna

whoever is without a home
when the fields grow dark

whoever sits in his lone room
when evening comes and cool

whoever felt the worst of wounds
when snow falls on the windowsill

whoever never grief-stricken nights
when the feeble candle flame

whoever in forests of flowers mountain chains
when I plucked the raging weeds from your mouth

whoever tiredly up to the host of stars
when from your looking I am deeply calmed

whoever knows only for others endures like a blindman
when the silvery moon shines through the thicket

whoever looked on beauty with his eyes
when numbers and figures no longer

whoever is condemned to separation from beauty
when the eyes break

whoever never ate his bread with tears
if it were not for hope

stille post

[Translator's note: This poem is a montage of famous lines from German poetry; the original poem appears below, along with the source of each line in parenthesis.]

hosianna

wer jetzt kein haus hat (Rilke)
wenn die felder sich verdunkeln (Dehmel)

wer einsam sitzt in seiner kammer (Novalis)
wenn der abend kommt und kühle (folk song)

wer die tiefste aller wunden (Günderode)
wenn der schnee ans fenster fällt (Trakl)

wer nie die kummervollen nächte (Goethe)
wenn die leichte kerzenflamme

wer in der blumen wäldern bergesreihen
wenn ich das tollkraut dir vom munde pflückte

wer ermüdet hinauf zu der heerschar der gestirne (Klopstock)
wenn ich von deinem anschaun tief gestillt (Mörike)

wer für andre nur weiss der trägt wie ein blinder
wenn der silberne mond durch die gesträuche blickt (Hölty)

wer die schönheit angeschaut mit augen (Platen)
wenn nicht mehr zahlen und figuren (Novalis)

wer von der schönen zu scheiden verdammt ist (Goethe)
wenn die augen brechen (Brentano)

wer nie sein brot mit tränen ass (Goethe)
wenn die hoffnung nicht wär (folk song)

epilogue to *stille post*

confusion—that is the stylistic principle of the poem. anarchy is the
order of our life. it is the order of the poem. its materials are
fragments of folk songs, clichés, march music, and trivialities. the
voice of the people is the voice of the poem. but what everyone says
so easily—is here dismantled, mutilated, broken down into pieces.
every line is amputated. the dissecting scalpel is the question: ques-
tioning, i interrupt the voice of the people. what is known to all—is
now no longer recognizable. doubt about generality? generality
swallows the doubt! the collective remains victor over the individ-
ual. thus i dispense with everything private, emotional, differenti-
ated. i dispense also with my own personal opinion. there remains:
a scrapbook in which are collected snapshots from the mind-states
of the people. there remains: a museum in which are displayed the
dried-up trophies of the indestructible. to destroy the indestructi-
ble—that is the paradox of the poem.

BARBARA FRISCHMUTH

Barbara Frischmuth (1941–   ) is one of the leading younger prose writers in Austria today. Associated with the Graz Authors and the "Forum Stadtpark," she first attracted attention with her short-prose work *Die Klosterschule* (Frankfurt: Suhrkamp, 1968) and has since made a name for herself in the line initiated by Peter Handke. The poem below, from the journal *manuskripte* (1982), is one of her few published nonprose works, wherein the narrative tendency is nevertheless evident.

My Chinese Summer

Little rain clouds from Yunnan-Tee
Sun through a straw hat
the artful forms in which the world
comes to rest for a moment
in the shadow of unrest   its penetration
the inevitable decay and
the repeated search for connection
spirit-thresholds for the fighter   a stumbling
fear lames the breath   disorderly retreat
the simple question: is there enough for all to eat
expectation and hope: we're working on it
in its broken form: from rice alone
cautious yes: the benevolent commissioning of a street drain
corresponding no: the omnipresence of control
how little may be said in order not to endanger how much

Between heaven and earth we hang wind-sons
exposed to air currents   left to fall like sand

from the Gobi that sinks on Peking's streets
the simple things with their complicated backgrounds
a thermos bottle a mat and bedding for a change
a bowl of noodle soup is one form of satiety
the other roasted queen-bees in Szemau
people squat when brushing their teeth at the fountain
over hibiscus branches hang soaplessly laundered suits
manifestation of desired form
a tree that conforms to its image   fish
with deliberation transformed over centuries into ornamental
    fish
radish cut to chrysanthemum
an art object and we eat from it
love counts as one of the most secret joys
but eye language has not been lost

The old and the new meaning of mandate
from heaven   the consequences of natural disaster
on the charisma of the current ruler
THE SUPERIORITY OF NOT WANTING   questions
about questions to LAO DSE   how he can be grasped
in the mutually contradictory translations
THE WHOLE WORLD KNOWS: WEAKNESS
    OVERCOMES STRENGTH
                              MILDNESS
    OVERCOMES RIGIDITY
BUT NO ONE PUTS IT INTO PRACTICE
obstinacy in the small things   the court land
that bears much more fruit than the fields of the brigades
by the Golden Path at the edge of the irrigated rice fields
a four-leafed clover and everybody believes in it
the all-encompassing regard for the body
rest as insight into its necessity
still dipping into the residuum of wisdom
the mouth of the new one occasionally runs over
what remains are the figures of script   crow's feet
in the corner of the eye   millennia of history

a small monkey with pointed cap   king
and well-liked by his laughing subjects
my belt stayed in Canton where I absent-mindedly
looked at it in my Chinese summer

manuskripte

PETER HANDKE

Peter Handke (1942–   ) scarcely needs introduction, since he is recognized as perhaps the leading writer in Austria today. After a dramatic debut with *Publikumsbeschimpfung* in 1966, he wrote further works for the stage, but narrative prose emerged as his primary mode of expression in the 1970s and 1980s, with a new title added almost every year. He also writes poetry, as represented by *Die Innenwelt der Aussenwelt der Innenwelt* (1969) and the selections below, which are drawn from a recent volume of diverse texts entitled *Das Ende des Flanierens* (1980), both titles at Frankfurt: Suhrkamp.

Métro Balard-Charenton

At sundown I got in
at Motte-Piquet-Grenelle
At Bonne Nouvelle I stopped
to page through the pariscop
At the Filles du Calvaire station
the coke machines were empty
At Daumesnil shoes were on display in a show case
Before Porte Dorée I still saw light
coming through a shaft
In Charenton-Ecoles
—where the Marne flows into the Seine—
it was already night
In the clear western sky somewhere
"Young Mr. Lincoln" was playing

Das Ende des Flanierens

Occasional Poem

Finally toward midnight
the boys come home from the movies
with new pop-talk
and the tired parents on the couch
laugh with them submissively

Das Ende des Flanierens

The Course of a Day in a Summer Garden

A few leaves fell this afternoon
from the acacia plant
And at evening the lamp swayed
in the empty dining room

Das Ende des Flanierens

Farewell in the Basilica

Face drifting away—motley grimace!
In the image of that moment
you were lost forever
suggesting the mask
with bones instead of cheeks
and slits instead of eyes
But the stone floor under my feet,
the flat stones bring you closer again
Absorbed in thoughts of stone
I weight us down with them

Beautiful burden of our heads
Never again do I want to see masks

Das Ende des Flanierens

Austrian Poem 1979/80

1. In a poem two otherwise separate things are brought together.
   A poem is a proclamation

2. Now!
   And the morning light in the elderbush

3. The acacia branch, whirled as a peace bough in the autumnal sky

4. Yesterday in the train the novel "Suddenly like a Stranger"
   Today on the snowfield a far-off rustling
   that was suddenly near-by

5. Sometimes it's hard to look at a snowman
   But a child goes up the stairs with a lively gait

6. In the morning in the perfume-cloud of a rural policeman
   In the afternoon the humor of a shiny cow-pie

7. A train whistle in the evening far away in the plain
   closes the inner self that was open during the day

8. The setting sun makes the edge of a mountain visible
   and behind the tamarack the moon appears:
   One thing leads to another
   and a person is happy

9. One thing leads to another
   and a person is happy:
   and the happiness leads to something else

10. The white face of a titmouse
    as a flake in twilight

11. Sulfur butterfly here
    yellow booklet dangling
    from the blue shirt there

12. Behind the town of Magnolia in the Alaskan Yukon
    the moon rolls as paddle wheel

13. Still in the morning a mild survey
    of the swastikas
    In the evening
    the moment of philosophy

14. "By 'good' I mean here any kind of happiness
        and further anything that leads to happiness"

15. "By 'reality' and 'perfection'
        I mean one and the same thing"

16. I think with enthusiasm
        but missing the love
        I want to write a poem for you

Das Ende des Flanierens

PETER HENISCH

Peter Henisch (1943–   ) is interested in sociopolitical issues, toward which he takes a critical stance, at once humorous and aggressive. While using some of the reductionist techniques of "experimental poetry," his concern with the communicability of a message separates him from that movement. Selections are from *mir selbst auf der spur* (Baden: Grasl, 1977).

everything is
in order folks
everything is
quite okay
everything is
in order folks
everything's
OK

don't look either
to the right or to the left
always stay comfortably
in the middle
watch TV or
go in for sports
then you won't get
any stupid ideas

everything is
in order folks
everything is
quite okay
everything is

in order folks
everything's
OK

don't ask questions
think about your blood-
pressure tend to
your own business
in light of eternity
what's the problem
in fifty years
it'll all be over

mir selbst auf der spur

in protest

against government policies
I demonstratively leave
my shoe lace untied

if I stumble
and sprain my ankle

it will (I think) become clear
what could happen

mir selbst auf der spur

your cage
(said the caretaker)
only SEEMS too small

because you always
go too close
to the bars

mir selbst auf der spur

you're right
I chase after myself

I am thus strictly speaking
running away from myself

but as long as I can
run away from myself

I must actually be
ahead of myself

(said the cat and continued
to play with its tail)

mir selbst auf der spur

ERNST NOWAK

Ernst Nowak (1944–   ) lives in Vienna, where he completed his university studies by writing a dissertation on Franz Kafka. He works in the rare-book trade, a thriving business in Austria, and writes novels and radio plays as well as poetry. Translations are from *Entzifferung der Bilderschrift* (Baden: Grasl, 1977).

sooner or later they will go in
and close the gate behind them

as if it got out of their hands
it will roll on its track
with such force
that nothing can hold it back
crashing
it will throw itself into the lock

they will settle down inside
in the twilight

as pale spots
they will stand out
from the weakly reflecting
black walls
they will peer into the void
without noticing
footsteps and gestures

oblivious of all
they will neglect themselves

shrivel up
already
half unreal

Entzifferung der Bilderschrift

I let a stranger
stay here once
for a night
since then
he lives here with me
in a corner

we don't say much
sometimes we laugh
and he says
some day he will be the boss here
then he will finally get rid of me
and finally he will be able to sleep

he who laughs last laughs best
he says
and sinks back with a groan
crumpled over
on his bed

now
I think
he will finally go to sleep
finally I will be able to sleep

but I hear
how he rolls around
grinding his teeth
smacking his lips
and how he sits up

when I sit up
and look over
I see
how he's looking at me

but some day
I say to myself
I will really be the boss here
then I will finally get rid of him

he who laughs last laughs best
I remember
and lie down again
with my face to the wall

Entzifferung der Bilderschrift

that knife
has stabbed me in the eye a long time
for a while I hesitated
but today I thought
now or never
and secretly
I searched through your pockets
and all the drawers

believe me
I didn't want to steal it
I didn't want it
I only wanted to inflict this wound
only this one cut
and only with this knife
your knife had to be the one
with which I cut myself

so that I
maliciously and shrewdly
could say
your knife is to blame
it was your knife
yours
you're to blame
just so you know
it was your knife

Entzifferung der Bilderschrift

PETER TURRINI

Peter Turrini (1944–   ) is well-known and popular as a playwright. His poetry cycle presents an "autobiographical" account of his childhood and youth, which is used to demonstrate the "normal catastophe" and the "repressiveness of the ordinary." Selections are from *Ein paar Schritte zurück* (München: AutorenEdition, 1980).

As a boy
I sometimes lifted
a chair
with my teeth
in hopes
that my weaknesses
would be disproved
by such strength.

Today, lacking good teeth,
I don't lift
chairs any more.
But the technique
of showing strength
so that weakness
will be overlooked
remains.

Ein paar Schritte zurück

How much longer
will I swallow everything
and act
as if nothing had happened?

How much longer
will I feign an interest in others
and with this friendly pose
ignore myself?

How much longer
do they have to hit me
before this silly smile
goes away?

How much longer
do they have to spit at me
before I show
my true face?

How long
can a person
not like
himself?

It's so hard
to tell the truth
when you've learned
to get by
on friendliness.

Ein paar Schritte zurück

I would like
to love my enemies
until they break
under my love.

I would like
to forgive my beloved
until she despairs
at her failures.

I would like
to help my friends

until they comprehend
their inadequacies.

I would like by all means to be a good man.

Ein paar Schritte zurück

I can understand
why you need so much time for everything.
I can understand
that you can't sleep with me tonight.
I can understand
why you cheat on me.
I can understand
that you want to be alone now.
I can understand
that you can't understand me.

My understanding for you
had enormous proportions.
With this power
I tried
to suppress you.

Ein paar Schritte zurück

The worst is
that I don't know
whether your affection
gives life
or takes it away.

When everything in me grows tense,
one thing remains:
You are to blame
with your obtrusive ability
to love me.

Ein paar Schritte zurück

I am not I.
In search of myself
I tear out my hair
break open my skull
dislocate my joints
cut up my chest.

At the end of this activity
there will be a pile of flesh
roughly thirty centimeters high
lying in front of me
and again I will not
be myself.

Ein paar Schritte zurück

The No
that I always wanted to say
has been thought a hundred times
quietly formulated
never articulated.

It burns in my stomach
takes my breath away
is ground between my teeth
and comes out
a friendly Yes.

Ein paar Schritte zurück

If I wanted to be satisfied
I would have to lose weight;
since I can't stick it out
I am dissatisfied.

If I wanted to feel fulfilled
I would have to write more;
since I don't get beyond beginnings
I feel unfulfilled.

If I wanted to be healthy
I would have to stop drinking;

since I continue to stagger home
I am very unhealthy.

If I wanted to use my time well
I would have to be more organized;
since I keep putting things off
the time gets away from me.

When I become
slim
sober
industrious
and organized
then my life will begin.

Until then I always feel guilty.

Ein paar Schritte zurück

PETER ZUMPF

Peter Zumpf (1944–   ) lives in his native city of Vienna, where he is associated with the *Podium* literary circle. His poetry, prose, and plays often demonstrate a satiric "suburban" view of modern life. Selections are from *Klärungen* in the well-known series "Lyrik aus Österreich" (Baden: Grasl, 1980).

Tell me,
you visited
the circus?

You saw
crying lions
melancholy
brown bears
with
neurotic
complexes
frustrated crocodiles
and psychopathic camels?

Tell me,
you were
a guest
with a
press card
on that
planet?

Klärungen

Neatly
and well
ordered
the time
lies
in the drawer
classifying
life
in
transparent folders

It
is still
to be
worked through

But
for that
the
prebend
has
no time

Klärungen

Quietly
just for himself
he dreams
again and again
the dreams
of his youth
on narrowly
described
calendar pages

Everything seems
finished
and
closed

The rest
is only
waiting time

in the
storage room

Klärungen

Beginning
each day
like the previous one
I hope
not
to have to begin
the next one
like all the others

Thus
I begin
each day
like a new day
still
hoping

having
long forgotten
for what

Klärungen

REINHARD PRIESSNITZ

Reinhard Priessnitz (1945–   ) is an experimental writer of the second generation who with imagination and invention further develops the discoveries of the Vienna Group. He is also interested in philosophy, aesthetics, and linguistics, and writes creditable theoretical-critical essays on avantgarde art and literature. Selections are from *vierundvierzig gedichte* (Linz: edition neue texte, 1978).

tropic circle

three hundred bridges
from the snow-hurt
to the snow-heart
        & back again
in the pitch-black
luck-shamble-stream
up to the blood
        & back again
on a carpet
of swallows and straw
for the summer
        & back again
minus moon and waltz-beat
with the talking river
through the mouth
        & back again
on all eye-crags
wave slow-

ly and foam-over
                   & back again
three hundred hallo-
weened rainbows
now full of thorns
                   & back again
                   & back again

vierundvierzig gedichte

snowsong

if my mirror talks itself blind
the snowfall will wander
the shards of the sky
the vein of the night
plays its soft voice
tumbling in the bullrush
my ordering mirror
plays its soft voice
cock and hen
the speaking becomes
when it snows a winter
reaper and scythe
the heart a flake
its voice will become
a frosty ribbon
its ice a flower
glassy shards
of pulsating night
we will hatch
white cock white hen
under snowfall and snowfall
we will wander
my talking mirror
clanging questions
in the falling dream

vierundvierzig gedichte

trip

in the fragile fireland
of spring, my valley,
that gently warms us
and opens the buds
to our desire; through the summer
further, the meadow
freckled, there we stick,
resin on resin; in the half-
shadow of the fall after-
noon, through your hair,
that intones the words;
to a lapland of lip-
s, there, where fondly,
as flakes, the snow
drives us . . .

vierundvierzig gedichte

privilegium minus

again a dream-rider day,
and the ironlight melts.
my kingdom is a horse
one sits well on its throne.

without watchman the heavens peer
out of tiger eyes, like, well;
corals foam from some suns
and black doves

silently swing their hat.
we wear the crown of wind
like the esteem of the city;
our journey, as rose,

multileafed, it blooms wherever
we go, queen aberration,
with thorns, the dew from our lips
freshens the land of tomorrow;

and land-tongues, detected, fly
apart and dissolve,
and fly like birds
orientally along the coasts.

that your wingbeat were my hoofbeat,
i dream and goad the spur
that drives us, as iron in light,
that is riding me

and melts like the throne;
constant remains only the aberration,
over there the birds are singing
and the morning is beautiful.

vierundvierzig gedichte

"white horse song"

white clock (?) white commu
nion (?) or when everything (?)
is revealed thus questions (?) &
early & the last face is ex
tinguished (?) with that what i
say say with that what i
(white mouth? white hand of the
clock i ask the time or when
everything is extinguished with
that what i) white (?) bouquet of
violets (?) tongue-white light
(?) where they hesitate (?) per
haps everything is closed up (?)
& confounded & generally early
(? white tongues & violets so
hesitating so light so at first
? & a little bouquet of light is ex
tinguished or is revealed time
ly with that what i) white
time (?) & opens its lips
or what do i say (?) it is
a morning broken & whole
so-to-speak i say & not once
(?) that with which what i (white
meadows? & what? what? when i
i so fearful what? & what? &
in general good morning) so
white & white & white but not
even time or that (?) & how
how i fail with that what i

know or say or fear or
when everything is extinguished or
when everything is revealed

vierundvierzig gedichte

[Translator's note: The poem rests on the multivalence in German of the word *weiss:* (1) as
adjective signifying the color "white," connoting innocence and purity; and (2) as a verbal form
in the first and third person singular meaning "to know," in both a cognitive and a sensory way,
with the derivative adjective *weise,* "wise."]

innery

minemyme but where
minemyme but where
the stone falls here or today but where
your dress & your hair & your hair where
but black or white or not or al-
ways where the water on the way that lets
& the ship & the foam & the keel where
but sofar the wideness widens
the eye but where the hand & the hand
& left or right but where the
evening comes whereas little &
much much more than the morethan but where much
more than the stone falls here or today but
where where but tomorrow he or he or he or
you you but you but you or yours or fromyours
while to while you but from where & where from
you yours your you yoursyouryou
and so on hehishimhe but
where on & so or so or then
not here & not her & water on
keelfoamship of the left hand to the right
ititsit so on & so   on
& so-on & so-on &&& the or you we
theirstheirthem & not on or not or so
but your hairdress or blackor white
& white and white but not me but where
he & he & he & he & my yes—
will & she & she or you
or not from where & from you
& wherefrom yes will & from

where & where & where & where
from where & from
where

vierundvierzig gedichte

plan for understanding

well & whatever on whatever in whatever
& again whatever behind whatever what
everwhatever yesyesy about whatever to whatever
above whatever at whatever whatever &
while whatever where whatever so whatever
between whatever & whatever beside or
whatever also whatever after whatever after

according to: you yawn, what? with with with with with
& whaterror & whaterror whenerror whaterror
under whaterror so but whaterring well clear
whaterror inviewof until whaterror or
& yes on whaterror out whaterror yes or
so togetherwith atfirst because & then again
or to or whaterror over or over or

whatever yesyesyesyes accordingto inconsequenceof but wh-
atever whatever whenever whoever
whatever or but under whomever & so &
against against & between whatever well therefore
so so & between hisever herever up
up! well whatever whatever dummy what-

ever or on or under or with or out of
or alongside or against or or or or
whatever without whatever between whatever
yes about becauseofwhatever forthesakeofwhatever ofwhatever
through whatever whatever hence whatever hence hence
whatforever whatnever because never be-
causeever & whatever always whatever well clear

vierundvierzig gedichte

PETER ROSEI

Peter Rosei (1946–   ) writes short lapidary poems (the designation has been questioned!) that present deceptively simple phenomenological "snapshots" of everyday occurrences. These stand in contrast to the narrative prose works for which the author is also known, and the entire production is not so "harmless" as it may initially appear. He holds a degree in law but lives as a free-lance writer in Salzburg. Selections are from *Regentagstheorie: 59 Gedichte* (1979) and *Das Lächeln des Jungen: 59 Gedichte (1979)*, both at Salzburg: Residenz.

Foreword to *Regentagstheorie*

What interests me about the poem is self-forgetting speech. In that I look at the world, I speak about it. I speak already in that I look at it. In the looking I overlay my field of vision with signs, meanings. What I call self-forgetting speech is a speaking in the language. In this speech the speaking recedes. It is not interesting. Yet the speaking wants to present itself. It presses toward the spoken. It sneaks in. Thus I come into the poem. Thus *my* meanings come into the poem. What I wanted, fails. Of course: It had to be that way. That is no consolation.

     The car goes slowly around the curve, now
     the curve is empty, it lies in the sunshine,

nearby the shadow of the tree, the leaves
still sway from the car that went by.

Regentagstheorie

The whistling flew around the corner; it had
wings of tin; it was a lit-
tle hole in the afternoon. The man who
had whistled it threw back his
head. He looked up at the buildings;
the pavement shone silently; it was
as if it had just rained.

Regentagstheorie

From the meat of books I ate with pleasure. I was
young. Everything smelled good and was ruddy!
I don't know how to live, never learned it.
How white the books are! The snow.

Regentagstheorie

Grass shines in the wind;
more gently it goes through the
streets; it touches on open
shutters. Brooms sweep
leaves into the gutter, where
rain water had swelled, then
quickly disappeared. Now the
pavement is already dry.

Regentagstheorie

At the stand where we ate fish
a man looked in who had diagonal

slits in his eyes, high rocks
were behind him, we slept through
the afternoon that was full of honey.

Das Lächeln des Jungen

The man sits at the table
with a bottle, the flowers in the
vase are high, up to his chin, he
doesn't see them, looks instead
at the next table, where a woman
sits eating with her husband.

Das Lächeln des Jungen

The barn is full of mice. The
cat climbs around as if he had
boots on. My heart aches, it's
not the sadness. The cat has
a red collar. He belongs to
the blond lady, who in turn
belongs to a man, who sometimes
lives there with her in the empty cottage.

Das Lächeln des Jungen

Your love is like fire, croons the
voice on the radio. In the frying pan
freshly-broken fried eggs sizzle
in fat that forms brown bubbles.

Das Lächeln des Jungen

The Standing Woman

As if her face were made of glass! She
stands there erect, resolute, ready
to go; doesn't go however and remains
in the open door where the day, through
which colored birds fly, looks in.

Das Lächeln des Jungen

Name Index